Nine Roads to the Battle of New Orleans

Nine Roads TO THE BATTLE *of* NEW ORLEANS

RYAN STARRETT

FOREWORD BY MIKE BUNN

Published by The History Press
An imprint of Arcadia Publishing
Charleston, SC
www.historypress.com

First published 2025

Manufactured in the United States

ISBN 9781467170376

Library of Congress Control Number: 2025943930

To the team at Aquinas Writing Advantage, led by Professor Erin M. Brown, MA, MFA. Thank you for the opportunity to teach the next generation of writers and for designing the curriculum that won back to back to back iLearn Awards, recognizing the top online writing program in the country.

CONTENTS

FOREWORD

The Battle of New Orleans will forever remain a landmark event in American history. It is remembered as the definitive end of the War of 1812, a fight that helped our young nation begin to remove European colonial powers from its contested Gulf Coast region and the one conflict above all others that made an ambitious middle-aged general by the name of Andrew Jackson a household name and military hero. Its effects would and still do ripple through our shared heritage.

But the sheer audacity of the victory—one of the most lopsided of our nation's many illustrious military feats—lingers in our collective understanding of its fighting. It was a complete and devastating triumph, a pageant of destruction played out on a relatively compact battlefield, which visitors today can visualize relatively easily. On one side of the battlefield stood what many viewed as the most fearsome military force on the planet at the time, the British army, which would best even the renowned Napoleon. Confronting them from the other side of the field was a hastily cobbled-together and unevenly equipped assemblage of men from diverse ethnic and cultural backgrounds who had never before worked together. All that stood between the two, with the fate of the vital trading center of New Orleans—and perhaps that of the larger region for the immediate future—hanging in the balance was a crude, ad hoc line of defenses thrown up along an old millrace in a muddy field alongside the mighty Mississippi River. That the Americans would prevail was unlikely and unexpected; that they would crush their opposition and turn that field into a killing ground was utterly shocking.

Out of this showdown would emerge a number of stories of personal experiences that forever color our remembrance of the events of the famed "Glorious 8th of January." There is the bold maneuvering of the British army and navy officers leading to the fight on land and water; the gutsy gamble of a nighttime assault by Jackson to slow their progress; the superhuman valor and grim determination of the foes during that terrible, final showdown. All these comprise an extraordinary tale with thousands of individual strands well worth remembering and retelling anew in each generation.

There is a considerable body of literature on the battle, the overwhelming majority taking the shape of personal journals, biographies, and narrative histories of varying lengths, readability, and comprehensiveness. Several of the best of these, ranging from early accounts to the most recent scholarship, inform the fine work contained here by my friend Ryan Starrett. He is a seasoned writer, with several titles on Gulf Coast history, either authored or coauthored, already under his belt. In the pages that follow, Ryan does something no previous chronicler of the Battle of New Orleans has done. By following the personal sagas of nine key individuals associated with the contending armies—some familiar figures in the story of the battle and others who are likely new to many readers—he enables his audience to grasp not only the reality of the fight but also the backgrounds of the men who made history at Chalmette and how they ended up on opposite sides of this milestone event.

A cross-section of the leading officers, enlisted personnel and volunteers are all included, each receiving a biographical account. These narratives unfold in unison and collectively bring a new perspective to this most essential of American stories. It makes for a profoundly personal account of a complicated military campaign, which many will discover is much more multifaceted than they might have thought. The context, opposing strategies, mental and physical anguish, as well as the sound and fury of battle are related in an unfolding story that tracks real people whose actions bore real consequences. In documenting these individual narratives and bringing them to life in this unique way, Ryan has added another layer to a legend that still resounds today. *Nine Roads to the Battle of New Orleans* makes a special contribution to the historiography of the battle that is its focus, and it is a work that those interested in the battle's story will, without doubt, find both entertaining and enlightening.

Mike Bunn
Daphne, Alabama
January 2025

DRAMATIS PERSONAE

Andrew Jackson

After being abused by the British as a teenager during the American Revolution and left an orphan, Andrew Jackson lived a carefree and reckless life before settling down as a lawyer in Nashville, Tennessee. There, Jackson climbed the political ladder and held several prominent positions of influence. When the Red Stick War and the War of 1812 erupted, the fiery militia commander was only too eager to take the field once again against the empire that had taken everything from him three decades before.

Arsène Lacarrière-Latour

A Frenchman of moderate means during the Reign of Terror and rise of Napoleon, Latour traveled to Saint-Domingue on family business. There, he found another revolution and even more bloodshed. Deciding to seek his fortune in the newly independent United States, Latour found himself fighting against his native land's chief rival in what many were calling the "Second American Revolution."

Peter Ellis Bean

A filibuster turned idealist, seventeen-year-old Bean joined the ill-fated expedition of Philip Nolan into Spanish Territory in 1801. Over the next thirteen years, he would go on an odyssey through the inferno of revolutionary Mexico. Bean would spend some of his time in hiding and more fighting with Mexican revolutionaries against imperial Spain, but he spent most of his time in various Spanish prisons. After a narrow and fortunate escape, Bean joined the forces of General Morales. In 1814, he was sent to the United States to garner support for the anti-imperial insurgents. In December 1814, Bean landed in New Orleans.

Daniel Todd Patterson

A lifelong Navy man, Patterson took to the seas at thirteen, hunting French privateers in the Caribbean. Four years later, he was a prisoner of the pirates of Tripoli. Once freed, Patterson resumed his career and was eventually given command of the naval station at New Orleans, where he would patrol the coast in search of pirates and smugglers. Ever zealous of his duty, Patterson often found himself in conflict with a dangerous nest of cult-like bandit-heroes known as the Baratarians. The arrival of the British in 1814 put his feud with the smugglers on hold.

Reuben Kemper

A giant in stature and personality, Kemper owned land on the United States–Spanish border in the Mississippi Territory. He also owned land on the Spanish side. Determined that *all* his land be considered American territory, Kemper fought the Spanish tooth and nail to hold onto his land while he and his brothers fomented rebellion after rebellion to free the coastal lands from the Spanish dons. Finally, after a decade of fighting, Kemper helped evict the Spaniards from Baton Rouge and Mobile, only to learn a new empire was threatening his recent gains.

Jean and Pierre Laffite

Smugglers, slave traders, and privateers, the brothers Laffite built a commercial empire in the swamps south of New Orleans. Vilified by the American government and condemned as "hellish banditti" by Andrew Jackson, the brothers were nonetheless viewed as heroes among New Orleans's Creole merchant class and the populace who profited from their lower-priced contraband. Courted by the British, the Laffites had to decide where to cast their die.

Edward Pakenham

Brother-in-law to the Duke of Wellington but a hero in his own right during the Napoleonic Wars, Pakenham was offered command of the British North American Army—a command turned down by his more famous brother-in-law. Pakenham accepted and sailed toward his new army, which was awaiting him in Jamaica, only to find his troops had already sailed to New Orleans, fought a battle outside the city, and were now mired down in a most disadvantageous position. Pakenham's talents and resolve were tested as he determined how best to extricate his army.

George Robert Gleig

The son of a Scottish bishop, Gleig left behind his own studies to enlist in the army of the Duke of Wellington. After participating in battle on the continent and seeing Napoleon exiled, Gleig continued his martial career across the pond. A gifted and perceptive writer, this former student was a participant in the Battle of Bladensburg, the burning of Washington, and the bombardment of Fort McHenry, recording his experiences and thoughts along the way. The Battle of New Orleans provided more than enough harrowing material for the insightful young Gleig.

Edward Nicolls

"Fighting Nicolls" earned his sobriquet 107 times over. The ultrareligious Irish Protestant began amassing wounds at the age of eleven, when he joined the Royal Navy. A devout abolitionist and proponent of Native rights, Nicolls was sent to the Gulf Coast to rally fifth columns of Natives and enslaved people to assist the British forces in the south. With customary aplomb, Nicolls embraced his new mission with zeal, assured that he was fighting for country, God, and the universal rights of mankind.

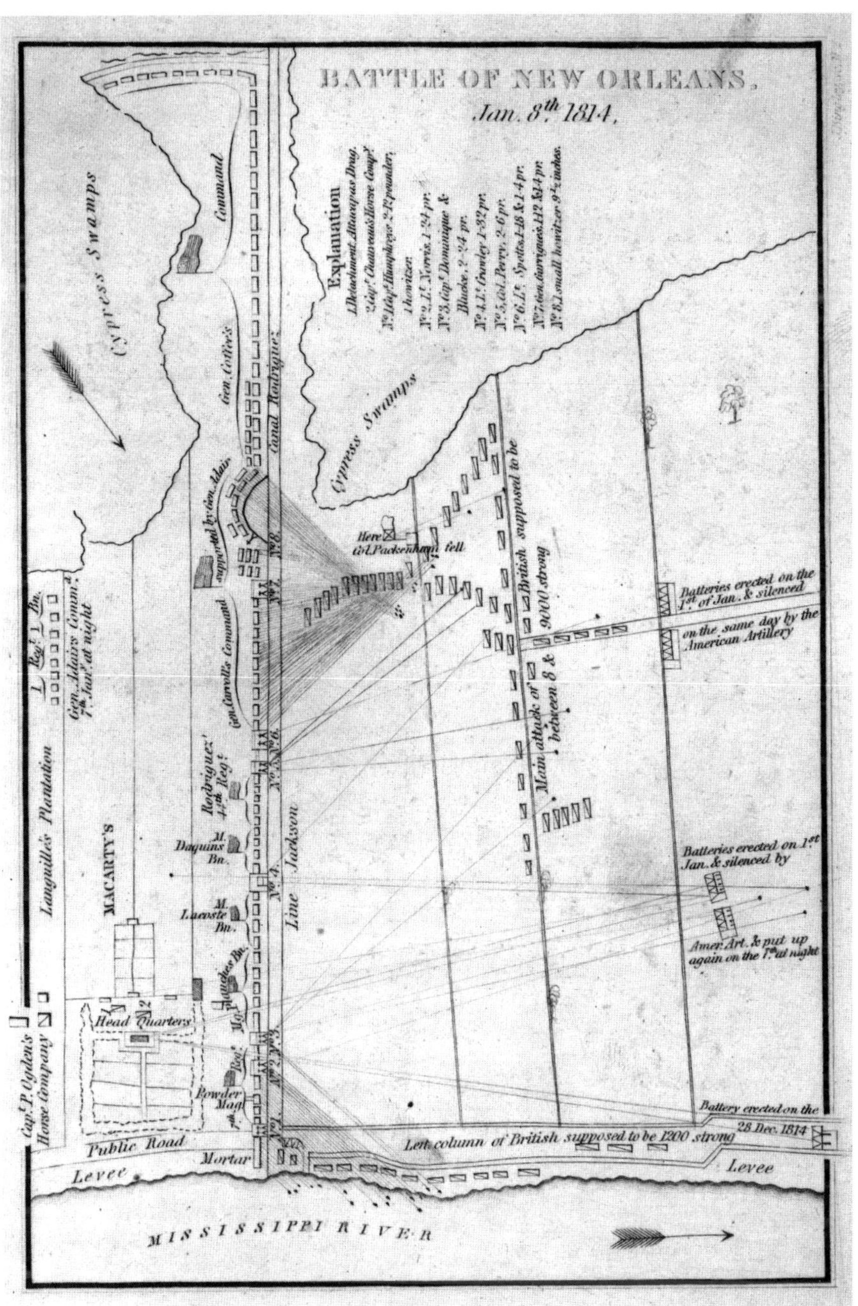

Map of the Battle of New Orleans. *Public domain.*

PART I

THE PRELUDE

1
THE MAKING OF AN ANGLOPHOBE

ANDREW JACKSON
1779–1781

His brother was dead. Hugh Jackson had fought at the Battle of Stono Ferry on June 20, 1779. He survived the battle, though wounded. He would not, however, survive his wound and the South Carolina summer sun, which dehydrated and then killed him. Twelve-year-old Andrew Jackson was heartbroken.[1]

Almost one year later, Jackson and his mother hurried to an impromptu hospital near their farm in the Waxhaw region of the Carolinas. A regiment of Virginia Continentals had been ambushed by British cavalry under Banastre Tarleton. When the Americans hoisted the white flag, the officer who bore the flag was promptly bayoneted, and a massacre ensued, in which 113 Americans were killed and another 203 were wounded. Tarleton returned to the main British force, leaving 150 severely wounded Americans on the field. It was these men whom Jackson and his mother rushed to help.[2]

The Waxhaw Massacre shocked the Deep South and provided a jolt for the Americans, as hundreds of recruits flocked to the Patriot cause. Among the most recent recruits were thirteen-year-old Andrew Jackson and his last living brother, Robert.

Because of his age, Andrew was assigned as an armed courier. After a successful first battle, the Jackson brothers were sent to a nearby Patriot house to await further reinforcements. When the local British commander learned of the Patriot presence, he surprised the house with Loyalist militia

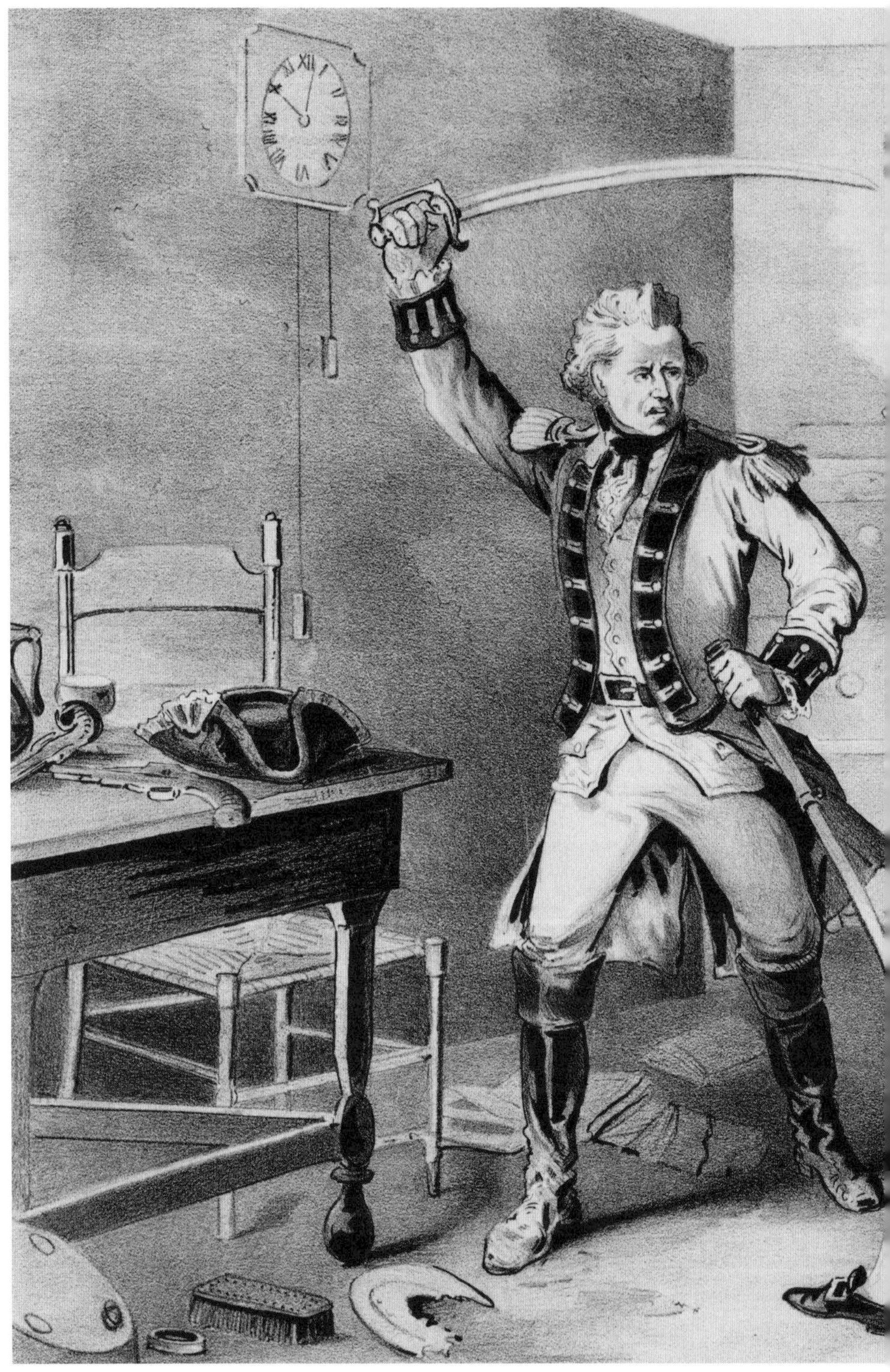

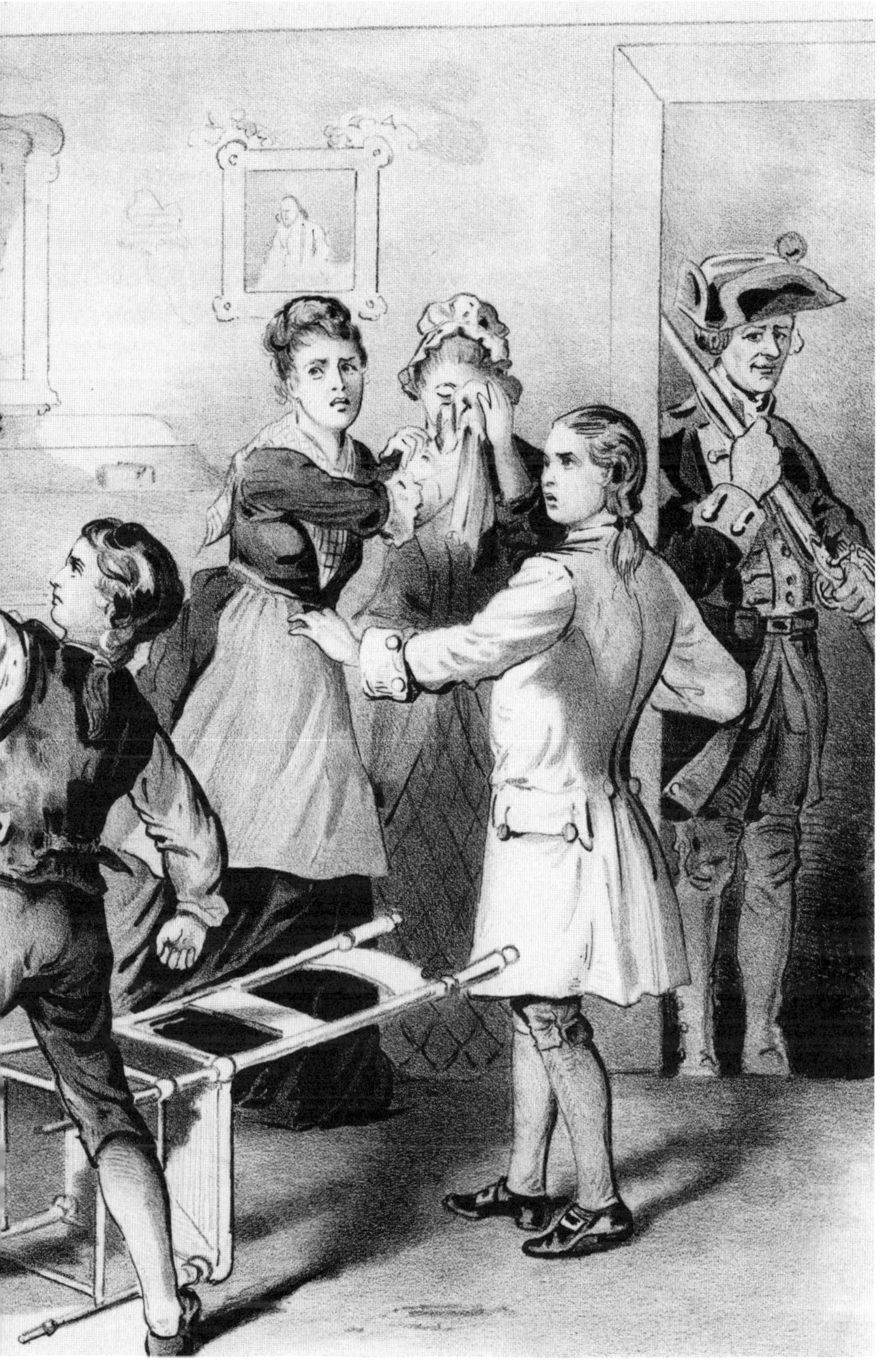

The Brave Boy of the Waxhaws, by Currier and Ives (1876). *Library of Congress.*

and mounted dragoons. Andrew and Robert fled into the swamps. The following morning, the brothers emerged from the swamp and made their way to their cousin's house. Ravenous, the pair had just sat down to breakfast when British dragoons stormed into the house and arrested the boys. Before marching the Jacksons off to prison, the British ransacked the house. The chief officer ordered Andrew to clean his muddied boots. When he refused, demanding to be treated as a prisoner of war, the officer swung his sword at Jackson's head. Jackson raised his left hand to protect himself, and the blade cut his hand to the bone and gashed his head. Then the officer turned to Robert and demanded the same. Robert, too, refused and was knocked unconscious.[3]

The wounded Jackson boys were then marched forty miles with no food and water to a makeshift prison. They were stripped of their coats and shoes and thrown into a cramped compound with 250 other Patriot prisoners, who had been subsisting on one ration of stale bread a day. Inevitably, disease quickly spread among the prisoners. Because of their untreated wounds, the two brothers quickly developed high fevers and chills and, like their older brother, Hugh, became dehydrated. Death was imminent.

Andrew's mother, Elizabeth, made her way to the prison and helped convince the British commanders to include her two boys in a prisoner exchange. In a pouring rain, the small caravan of released Patriots made their way back to the Waxhaws. Robert, now wracked by smallpox in addition to his festering wounds, was held in a saddle by his comrades. A barefoot Andrew walked behind in a fever-induced daze. When the trio arrived home, Elizabeth did everything in her power to keep her last two children alive. But Robert was too far gone. Two days later, he died. It seemed Andrew would soon follow. Tossing and turning, emitting the fumes of death from his infected and sore-festered body, Andrew seemed fated to join his father and two brothers in death.

And then the fever broke. His sores began to crust over. Andrew was on the slow road to recovery. He would remain in bed for months, but he would live.

Convinced that her youngest and last boy would survive, Elizabeth decided to travel to Charleston, where two of her nephews were being held aboard a British prison ship. Conditions there were worse than they had been in the Jacksons' prison, as cholera had broken out aboard ship. But Elizabeth was determined not to lose any more kin to this cursed war.

She went into Andrew's room, bade him goodbye, and, perhaps with a premonition of doom, advised him: "Make friends by being honest and keep them by being steadfast. Never tell a lie, nor take what is not your own, nor sue for slander—settle them cases yourself!"[4]

These were the final words Andrew Jackson's mother spoke to him. They were the final words any of his immediate family spoke to him. In November 1781, Andrew received a package. Inside were his mother's spare clothes and a message notifying him that his mother had died of cholera and was buried in an unmarked grave two hundred miles away.

At fourteen, Andrew Jackson was now an orphan, alone in the world.

2

CAPTURE

Peter Ellis Bean
March 22, 1801

Filibusters from a waxing United States had long had their eyes on the waning Spanish empire. St. Augustine and Pensacola were the primary targets, but men like Phillip Nolan looked to the lands west of the Mississippi River.

With the approval of Thomas Jefferson, the Natchez-based filibuster recruited fellow adventurers to make frequent trips with him across the border. The mission of the posse was to buy/capture wild mustangs. Nolan would also make contact with Native tribes and create maps of Spanish lands to the immediate west of the United States border. These maps would prove invaluable to now-President Jefferson and other American expansionists.

Eighteen-year-old Peter Ellis Bean had recently arrived in Natchez after the flatboat carrying his father's trade goods capsized and left the young voyager with little prospects. After arriving in Natchez, Bean fell under the charm of Nolan and decided to join the expedition with the hopes of making his fortune.

Bean suddenly awoke. The 18 men he had traveled with were now just 12, and 150 Spanish soldiers with their Native guides had surrounded his camp; 6 of Bean's companions had been taken at the corral they were supposed to defend.

Peter Ellis Bean, originally published in *A History of Texas for Schools*, by Anna Pennybacker (1907). *Internet Archive.*

It didn't matter. Phillip Nolan was still in command. These 12 Americans (including Black Caesar, an enslaved man) were more than enough to send 150 Spaniards flying.

And then a bullet pierced Nolan's head, killing him instantly. Two more Spanish bullets lodged in American bodies. Bean and his remaining companions returned fire from the horse pen. A mule-drawn Spanish cannon then made its debut, spewing grapeshot at the besieged company. Bean urged his comrades to charge the cannon with him. They demurred, deciding instead to retreat. The nine uninjured and two wounded loaded their weapons and filled their pockets with powder and shot. They placed the rest of the ammunition on Caesar and made for a ravine in the distance, running a gauntlet of lead, returning fire as they fled.

When given the chance, Caesar surrendered himself and the ammunition. One of the wounded filibusters did the same. Bean and his companions continued a firefight retreat. Eventually, the ten were pinned down and began exchanging a quickly dwindling supply of shots with the Spaniards. When the latter came forward under a white flag and offered the Americans the chance to simply return to the United States, Bean and company eagerly accepted the offer. As part of the deal, the Spanish would escort them to Nacogdoches and then send them on their way.[5]

When the group reached the Spanish outpost, the commandant told Bean he needed official word from his superior before he could free the Americans. One month later, Bean and his nine comrades were placed in chains and sent to San Antonio, where they would lie in prison another three months.

The next phase of their descent to Mexico City was a sixteen-month prison layover in San Luis Potosi. Fortunately for Bean, the authorities allowed him to sit outside his prison cell and mend shoes, which gave him the means to clothe himself and lay aside some money for future use.

But then it was time to move again, this time four hundred miles to the south, where the ten would finally be tried in Chihuahua. After five or six days in prison, Bean and his companions were told they were to remain Spanish prisoners. Only now, they would have free rein of the town and would be given the equivalent of a quarter dollar each day to feed and support themselves. Each night, they would report back to the barracks. Bean passed himself off as a hatter and employed a couple of locals to assist him. The ruse worked, and Bean was able to set aside a reasonable amount of money.

After four years of an ultra-lax confinement, most of Bean's compatriots accepted their fate and adjusted to life in Spanish Mexico. Bean, however, longed to return to the United States and began plotting to do so. Under the pretext of furthering his business, he was granted leave to visit a friend in a neighboring town. While there, he purchased four horses, three rifles, and six pistols and convinced his friend to flee with him.[6]

After hiding his materiel, Bean returned to Chihuahua and awaited the day of his auto emancipation. He wrote a letter to his comrade naming the day and place the two were to rendezvous. To Bean's dismay, the letter came into the hands of another filibuster, who opened the letter, read its contents, and, in the hopes of ingratiating himself with the authorities, handed it over, thereby denouncing his former comrade. Bean was promptly arrested and thrown into prison.

Three months later, Bean was again set at liberty under the same conditions he had enjoyed for four years as a hatter. He was soon granted permission from the commandant to visit a sick friend in a neighboring town. While there, he came across the man who had betrayed him. Bean challenged him

Chihuahua from the Casa de Moneda, by William Henry Jackson (circa the 1880s). *Library of Congress.*

to a duel, and when his betrayer refused, Bean ambushed him outside a house he frequented and beat him with a stick. The battered man pressed charges, but Bean was exonerated.[7]

Having spent five involuntary years in Mexico, Bean was more determined than ever to return to the United States. For five years, his case had languished in Spain. President Thomas Jefferson denied knowledge of their expedition and told Spanish authorities to prosecute the filibusters according to their own laws. Bean would later write of Jefferson: "This showed little humanity or feeling, thus to give us up to a nation more barbarous than the Algerines."[8]

Bean realized if he was to return home, it would be by his own wits and daring.

3

SAINT-DOMINGUE

Arsène Lacarrière-Latour September 1802–November 1803

Arsène Lacarrière-Latour was born in 1778 and consequently spent his formative years amid the bloody French Revolution. He trained to become an architect, but the chaos of the revolution slowed his studies. Then the rise of Napoleon and the consequent need for ever more soldiers pushed Latour into an early marriage in order to avoid the draft.[9] In 1797, Latour married Marie-Caroline de Montal, and less than two years later, the couple welcomed the first of their two children. Latour was now under pressure to provide for a family of three.

Fortunately, Marie-Caroline's great-uncle had left some profitable properties in Saint-Domingue to the Montal family. Part of Latour's marriage contract required him to "claim all the assets and rights of his bride."[10] And that was exactly what Latour planned to do.

In September 1802, Latour boarded a ship in Le Havre, France, destined for Cap-Français in French Saint-Domingue. The plan was for Latour to make his fortune and return to his young wife and family in Aurillac, France. Latour would spend the rest of his life as a wandering journeyman, offering his services to republics and kings across the United States and Caribbean. Latour would never see his wife again. He would see his children and native country only in the waning years of his life.

Latour's decision to move to Saint-Domingue was a gamble. A dozen years prior, Dutty Boukman, an enslaved man, overseer, and Voodoo priest inaugurated what would become the independent republic of Haiti—but only after a decade and a half of bloody wars and unspeakable betrayals, tortures, and horrors.

The Mamaloi in a Scarlet Robe, by Alexander King. First published in *The Magic Island*, by William Seabrook (1929), which details religious practices in Haiti. *Internet Archive.*

By the time Latour had landed in October 1802, the relative peace that had accompanied Toussaint Louverture's rise and subjugation of the island was in peril. The "Black Napoleon" and Napoleon had fallen out. Another slave rebellion had arisen in the northern end of the island. Louverture's repression was harsh, and Napoleon had sent an army of

thirty-four thousand men under the talented General Leclerc with the intent to place the valuable island firmly back under French control. When Louverture realized his position as de facto king of the island was imperiled, he ordered Cap-Français burned. So, when Latour landed, he saw devastation everywhere. Nearly half the buildings were burned, and the homeless, sick, and dying filled the streets beneath whatever squalid materials they could find.[11]

Leclerc's men recaptured much of the northern island and finally captured Louverture in September. They sent him back to France in chains, but the general's capture did not bring peace to the embattled island. In fact, Louverture's arrest led to more intrigue as rebel and slave commanders began jockeying for position. Overtures were made to the Spanish and British to aid the various Black forces. Soon enough, another civil war erupted, and massacres were reported by both sides all over the island. Latour surely second-guessed his decision to seek his fortune on the war-torn island.

That decision shifted from foolish to potentially fatal when a yellow fever epidemic ravaged the island. By the end of 1802, only eleven thousand soldiers of Napoleon's initial thirty-four-thousand-man force were still alive. And eight thousand of those men were in the hospital.[12] Understandably shaken by the events occurring all around him, Latour wrote home:

> *I finally arrived here after…a thankfully uneventful crossing, although badly bothered by the sea and hoping to get to land. But what an ill-omened reception! Having hoped to find things in good condition based on the news we had been given in France…I only found, to the contrary, that absolutely nothing was moving. Only shortly before our arrival, the blacks were on the verge of taking possession of the Cap. Fortunately, the national guard strongly repelled them.*[13]

Nevertheless, Latour had gone to Saint-Domingue to make his fortune. He promptly was made a member of the engineer corps, tasked with both rebuilding the island and saving it from further destruction.

Opposite: Toussaint Louverture (date unknown). *Library of Congress.*

Right: "Revenge taken by the Black Army for the cruelties practised by the French" (1805). *Library of Congress.*

On February 4, 1803, roughly one hundred days after Latour's arrival, two outposts at the Cap were taken by rebels, and the French guards were put to death. French troops drove off the insurgents, but two weeks later, the rebels were back, this time killing many in the local garrison and putting to death the inhabitants in a local hospital. A nearby English frigate, sent to pay respects to General Leclerc's replacement, sat by and watched the carnage as it happened. Order was restored soon enough, but Latour never forgave the British for their lack of aid.[14]

The news only grew worse. France and Britian were again at war less than three months later. The French position on Saint-Domingue had become untenable. The French commander reported to the home government that the insurgent forces had killed 62,481 white inhabitants and 26 of the 43 generals sent to restore order on the war-torn island.[15]

Nearly everyone on Saint-Domingue now recognized the inevitable: the island was destined to become the Western Hemisphere's first Black nation state. Terrified white and free persons of color began fleeing the island en masse. American and Cuban smugglers—among them, Pierre and Jean Laffite—made fortunes overnight.[16]

Latour soon joined the emigrants and set sail for Cuba. The engineer wanted to return home to France, but he could not go back empty-handed. Instead, after a few weeks on the Spanish island, he embarked for the land he would proudly call home for the next fourteen years: the United States.

4
THE BORDERLANDS

REUBEN KEMPER
1799–1804

Reuben Kemper was a large man in stature and in vision. He envisioned his Spanish land grant becoming part of the United States. He intended to once again be an American citizen.

Kemper had migrated to the Bayou Sara area, which was then under the control of Spain, to help his employer establish a store. John Smith was a Baptist minister and merchant. Smith hoped to link his stores in Ohio with a market in Spanish Louisiana. So, he sent his trusted employee, Reuben Kemper, south.

The move proved profitable to both, and Reuben quickly established himself, becoming a full partner with Smith and paving the way for two of his brothers, Nathan and Samuel, to join him. He bought a slave and land along the Mississippi River. Quickly, the Kemper brothers established themselves and built powerful contacts. Reuben loved the river and his new home land—just not his homeland. He desired to be American again.

But then came a debilitating setback with his original benefactor, John Smith.

Smith was anxious to return to Ohio, where a political future awaited him. He terminated his contract with Reuben and demanded his share of the profits and store.[17]

When Senator Smith moved to Ohio to take his legislative seat, he expected his dealings in Spanish Territory to be settled. He asked Governor Carlos de Grand Pré to go ahead and resolve the dispute between him and Reuben.

Bayou Sara, by Henry Lewis (1850s). *Internet Archive.*

Reuben, meanwhile, expecting the United States to take West Florida sooner than later, did his best to avoid arbitration. He made frequent trips to Natchez and New Orleans. Eventually, Grand Pré appointed adjudicators to decide the fate of Reuben's land. Among those appointed was Ira Kneeland, one of Reuben's enemies. In the end, the hostile council voted in Smith's favor. Reuben was ordered to pay Smith nearly $6,000 and vacate Smith's store. To assure compliance, Grand Pré gave Smith a writ for Kemper's own 240 acres. Reuben was given eight months to acquiesce and depart Smith's property.

Reuben was livid. He blamed Grand Pré for running a corrupt court and swore vengeance on Kneeland, whom he claimed was bribed and out for his timber. Reuben's hatred then extended to Spain itself. It was the Spaniards who had put him out of business and stolen his land.

And as one of his friends later asserted: "[Reuben's wrath] was always felt by those against whom it was directed."[18]

Despite his wrath, Reuben was still under orders to vacate his property within eight months. Reuben had no intention of doing so, and the eight months passed. In fact, his two brothers, Nathan and Samuel, began adding on to the house—a clear sign that they would not be leaving their Bayou Sara home.

Nearly a year after his decision—and at Smith's prompting—Grand Pré finally ordered that the Kemper house should be confiscated and the Kempers themselves removed.

June 13, 1804

Alexander Stirling and twenty Spanish militia—a number of them Americans who were happy to live south of the border—approached Reuben's barricaded house. Reuben was off conducting business in New Orleans. A dozen armed men in the house addressed the militia captain: they would not leave but intended to fight to defend their rightful property.

Stirling and his men withdrew and formed a loose cordon around the house. When Nathan Kemper learned a second militia had united with Stirling's, he and his supporters snuck out at night and made their way across the American border.[19]

When Reuben learned of the encounter between Stirling and his brothers, he wrote Stirling a letter warning him that his actions were illegal and that he and his brothers would do what was necessary to defend their rights and property.[20]

June 18, 1804

On June 16, three days after fleeing Stirling's militia, the Kempers were back at their Bayou Sara house. By June 18, they had gathered a larger number of followers and borrowed and confiscated guns in the neighborhood. They sat in the open, melting and casting bullets, careless of passersby who might notice. They were there to fight.

June 19, 1804

Stirling and fellow militia captain Vicente Pintado decided against assaulting the well-fortified and manned house. Instead, they patrolled the roads leading to the Kempers'. On June 19, they arrested a few of the Kempers' supporters. A deputy rode to the Bayou Sara bridge to take the prisoners into custody and bring them to Stirling's plantation. Just as the deputy arrived, Kemper supporters sprang their ambush, freed their comrades, and took the Spanish militia captive. The latter were immediately released after their guns were confiscated.[21]

June 25, 1804

Grand Pré offered the Kempers amnesty if they would simply leave Spanish Territory. They refused, and in response, Grand Pré ordered Stirling to either arrest or kill the squatters in the barricaded house. Stirling raised a posse of more than sixty men and surrounded the house. In the morning, the militia stormed the house, only to find the Kempers had slipped away in the night with all their guns and powder.[22]

They would be back.

July 2, 1804

Grand Pré issued a proclamation in which he called the Kemper brothers "pirates," "vagrants," and "rebels." He called for their immediate arrest should they ever step foot on Spanish Territory again. Reuben was included in the proclamation, despite having been in New Orleans during the recent confrontations. He was, after all, the leader of the family and the one his brothers looked up to. Grand Pré ordered patrols to keep an eye on both the Kemper house and the border, with orders to take any of the Kempers dead or alive should they be found in Spanish Territory.

The proclamation only incensed the brothers. They continued their sporadic, small-scale raids across the border, stealing whatever of value they could find, with a special emphasis on weapons, namely guns and swords. It soon became clear that the Kempers had a larger raid in mind.

AUGUST 7, 1804

With Reuben still in New Orleans, Nathan and Samuel gathered a small band and plotted their most daring raid yet. They would capture Stirling and other militia leaders and then quickly make their way to Baton Rouge, where they would kidnap Grand Pré and hold the governor hostage, demanding Baton Rouge as the price of his release. They would then hold the city until the United States could send troops to take control.

The brothers informed neither the United States nor their brother, Reuben.

On August 7, 1804, Nathan, Samuel, and twenty followers rendezvoused north of the border at Pinckneyville. The first phase of their plan was successful, and they captured their early targets. However, word reached

Westward Ho!, a study by Emanuel Leutze (1860). *Library of Congress.*

Grand Pré, and he stationed a picket outside Baton Rouge. The Kempers' hope for surprise had now dissipated. They exchanged shots with the pickets, wounding two Spaniards and sending the rest fleeing to the safety of the fort.

But Grand Pré outnumbered his adversaries and was protected by the walls of his fort. When he refused to negotiate with Nathan, the latter was forced to withdraw, eventually back north of the border.[23]

American renegades had now kidnapped foreign officers on foreign soil, fired on and wounded imperial troops, and staged a coup with the aim of capturing a Spanish city and its royal governor. There would be reprisals.

Although Reuben had been in New Orleans and not involved in his brothers' recent plot, he would bear the blame. He was the leader of the Kemper brothers, and he retained that position and the admiration of his younger brothers when he returned to Pinckneyville. There, he bided his time until the conditions were right to reclaim his 240 acres at Bayou Sara.

The Spanish, too, bided their time.

All knew it was only a matter of time before Reuben Kemper made his next move.

Meanwhile, Grand Pré planned a preemptive strike.

5

A PRISONER IN TRIPOLI

DANIEL TODD PATTERSON
OCTOBER 31, 1803–JUNE 3, 1805

At thirteen years of age, Daniel Todd Patterson enlisted in the U.S. Navy in pursuit of adventure. By fourteen, he had become a midshipman. At seventeen, he stood aboard a doomed ship off the African coast and watched as swarms of pirates eagerly rowed toward his sinking ship.

The *Philadelphia* was stranded on an invisible shoal, twelve feet under water, just two miles from the shores of Tripoli. Midshipman Daniel Todd Patterson's disbelief turned to fear as he watched nine pirate boats approach his ship. An equally incredulous Captain William Bainbridge calmly ordered all cannons, weapons, and war materiel to be thrown overboard. It was no use fighting back. The awkward angle of the stranded *Philadelphia* caused some cannons to face skyward, others pointed down toward the Mediterranean Sea. Capture was inevitable. Bainbridge ordered holes drilled into the bottom of the ship. If he was going to surrender another ship to the enemy, he would surrender a ship so damaged as to be useless.[24] The captain, Patterson, and the crew of the doomed frigate then awaited the moment their captors swarmed over the tilted sides of their frigate.[25]

And swarm they did. After realizing the surrender was no ruse, the pirates advanced and quickly secured the *Philadelphia*. The Americans were relieved of their valuables and coats and forced to row the smaller boats to shore, with pirates "standing with drawn sabres over our heads."[26]

Immediately upon docking, Patterson and his fellow captives were marched through the streets of Tripoli to much jostling, spitting, and jeering. At last, he and his companions stood inside the bashaw's castle before a raised throne, where the tall, dark-bearded pirate king sat on his velvet and

"Desperate conflict of American seamen under Decatur, on boarding a Tripolitan corsair," Whitney and Jocelyn (engravers) (1855). *Library of Congress.*

jeweled throne wearing a golden silk robe with a white turban and two gold pistols and a saber hanging from his diamond-studded belt. The bashaw simply stared at his captives with a pleased and condescending expression.[27]

Without a word, Patterson and company were sent off. The next day, the officers were taunted by the Barbary High Admiral Peter Lisle, a Scotsman turned Barbary pirate. He wanted to know if Captain Bainbridge was a coward or a traitor: "Who with a frigate of 44 guns, and 300 men, would strike his colours to one solitary gunboat, must surely be one or the other."[28] The humiliated Bainbridge, along with Midshipman Patterson and the rest of the officers, was sentenced to an indefinite prison term.

Patterson and company were the lucky ones, for their confinement turned out to be nineteen months of de facto house arrest in a home overlooking the harbor.

The rest of the crew received what could prove a death sentence depending on the length of their captivity: forced labor building up the city walls. The crew were charged with moving large stones, weighing four to eight thousand pounds, via carts. The *Philadelphia*'s carpenter later reported: "We worked bare-headed and bare-footed. Our necks were burnt to a perfect blister."[29] Their food was meager and their clothes tattered. With the daily whippings, many of the crew began to waste away.

Patterson and the officers were forced to watch their companions wither away day after day. Captain Bainbridge wrote to his wife: "It would have been a merciful dispensation of Providence if my head had been shot off by the enemy, while our vessel lay rolling on the rock."[30]

On February 16, 1804, three and a half months after Patterson and company were captured, American sailors conducted a daring raid in which they set fire to the docked *Philadelphia*, thus depriving the bashaw of a valuable weapon in his war against the Americans.

No doubt, the officers rejoiced to see the demise of the *Philadelphia*. However, the daring raid had harsh consequences for the ship's crew. The bashaw had been negotiating the end of the conflict and was using the prisoners as a bargaining chip. With the destruction of his newest pirate ship, the bashaw was in a vengeful mood. Crewman William Ray later recalled, "[L]ike so many fiends from the infernal regions, [they] rushed in among us and began to beat everyone they could see, spitting in our faces, and hissing like the serpents of hell.... [E]very boy we met in the streets, would spit on us and pelt us with stones; our tasks doubled, our bread withheld, and every driver exercised cruelties tenfold more rigid and intolerable than before."[31]

With negotiations now at a standstill, the fate of the *Philadelphia*'s crew seemed destined: slow, agonizing deaths as enslaved laborers of the Barbary pirates.

The fate of Patterson and his fellow officers, though certainly more comfortable than that of the crew, appeared equally bleak.

But then on April 27, 1805, a one-thousand-man army composed of Greeks, Muslims, and Americans won an improbable victory over an army of four thousand Tripolitans entrenched at Derna, an important fortified city east of Tripoli.

In the aftermath of the Battle of Derna, Bashaw Yusuf offered to release Bainbridge, Patterson, and their fellow prisoners for $200,000. The United States' consul general to the North African Coast, Tobias Lear, needed a diplomatic victory and offered $60,000 instead. On July 3, the bashaw accepted Lear's offer, and the prisoners were released after nineteen months of captivity.[32]

Back in the United States, the *National Intelligencer* proclaimed: "Our captive countrymen have been restored to the bosom of their country, peace has been made on honorable terms.... We have got all we wanted."[33]

Patterson and his companions were freed, but the United States paid a steep price: the young nation had negotiated with pirates. (Nine years later,

"A perspective view of the loss of the U.S. frigate *Philadelphia* in which is represented her relative position to the Tripolitan gunboats" (early 1800s). *Library of Congress.*

another negotiation with a separate band of pirates would drastically alter the composition of Patterson's own fleet.)

The 117 prisoners of the *Philadelphia* returned home in mid-September to the cheers and adulation of the American people. After nearly two years in a Tripolitan prison, they were now fêted as heroes.

Determined to become the hero he was hailed as, the newly promoted Lieutenant Patterson was sent to the New Orleans Station, where he would patrol the Mississippi River and Gulf of Mexico for the next eighteen years.[34]

6
KIDNAPPED

Reuben Kemper
September 2, 1805

Pinckneyville, Mississippi

Governor Grand Pré was tired of living in the cramped fort at Baton Rouge. He much preferred to dine and sleep at his large, comfortable home in town. But he was on the Kempers' death list. They had already tried to kidnap him once and were doing whatever they could to foment a rebellion in his territory.

Ira Kneeland also despised the Kempers and consequently found his name on the same death list. So did Alexander Stirling. And Abram Horton. And Henry Flowers. And Minor Butler. And many more who lived along the borderlands. Though Americans by birth, many who lived under the line were content to live in Spanish Territory on account of Spain's relatively lax laws. Reuben and his brothers were viewed as rabble-rousers and miscreants. They threatened the stability of the region and disrupted land prices. So, a significant number of Americans, contentedly living under Spanish rule, decided to teach the Kempers a lesson. Grand Pré tacitly approved.[35]

Reuben had returned to Pinckneyville, where he planned to stay a while. He naturally stayed at his house, along with his brother Nathan and his family. His brother Samuel moved to the store, where he lodged for the duration of Reuben's stay.

Two other friends were visiting the night of September 2, 1805. After dinner and conversation, the crew retired to bed. By 11:00 p.m., all were sleeping, Reuben on a mattress on the floor of his bedroom. Someone shouted from outside. Reuben went to the door and hollered back, demanding to know the reason for the shout. A man answered that he was Reuben's friend Basil Adams. Reuben opened the door, and several men with drawn pistols and clubs forced their way in. They secured the room and began beating Reuben with fists and clubs. Stunned and battered, Reuben gasped, "I surrender." The posse dragged him outside, stripped him, and continued to beat him. One of the tormenters pulled out his knife and cut a deep gash across Reuben's face. Abram Horton then began stomping Reuben's face.

By now, the vigilantes had Nathan outside. He had been dragged out of his bed and thrown on the ground next to his brother. As he was being carried to the door, he saw his wife being thrown to the floor and a man shouting, "If the bitch utters another word, put her to death." He heard a thud and then silence. When he called to his wife, he was met with silence. Now, he begged his captors to see her. They refused, and when she tried to crawl out of the house to join her husband, she was dragged back inside.

Reuben and Nathan were then bound and gagged. Nathan's two boys tried to run to their father, but they and everyone else in the house were told they would be shot dead if they set one foot outside the home. The posse then marched the brothers off into the woods.[36]

Meanwhile, a second, smaller posse was dispatched to "arrest" Samuel Kemper, who was at the family store, in bed with a fever. The five-man posse stormed the building, beat Samuel in bed, pulled him outside with a noose around his neck, and dragged him 150 yards before they finally allowed him to stand and race alongside the horse deeper into the forest.[37]

Reuben and Nathan were taken to the house of Abram Horton, just north of the border. Along the way, the men took turns periodically punching Reuben's face, certain they had pulled off a successful kidnapping and laughing as the blows landed.

Soon, Samuel's captors arrived with their prisoner, and the reunited posse crossed the border.

Just as they sauntered across the line, they stumbled upon a Spanish patrol.

"Are you Captain Alston?"

"Yes."

"The three Kemper brothers are prisoners."

"Come closer, *muchachos*."[38]

The vigilantes rode all three captives across the border, still bound and gagged, and then disappeared into the woods.

Planter's Cabin in East Baton Rouge Parish, Louisiana. It was originally built around 1800. *Library of Congress.*

Captain Solomon Alston took the three Kempers into custody and took them to a bayou nine miles distant, where a pirogue was already waiting to take them to Baton Rouge and Grand Pré.

No one bothered to disguise themselves now.

Reuben Kemper recognized all.

And he would never forget.

As the pirogue neared Baton Rouge, the beaten, bound, and gagged Reuben hatched a plan.

He signaled to his captor that he had something to say. Reuben was ungagged, and he asked if he might speak with a plantation owner, as he had an ongoing business deal. The guard agreed, despite orders to keep careful eyes on the brothers and the recent precautions he had taken in binding the trio together.

As soon as the pirogue was within range, Reuben began shouting: "We are the Kempers taken on the other side of the line, and these Spaniards are taking us prisoners to Baton Rouge!"[39]

Unknown to Reuben's captors, the man he had just hailed was attached to the U.S. garrison at Point Coupee five miles away. The American immediately saddled his horse and rushed to Point Coupee, where he informed the commandant that U.S. citizens had been kidnapped and were on their way to Spanish justice at Baton Rouge.

Lieutenant William Wilson, U.S. Army, pursued the Spanish pirogue and forced its surrender. Aboard, he found the three Kempers and a contingent operating on behalf of Spain. Flummoxed, Wilson wrote Governor Robert Williams of the Mississippi Territory and was told to send all aboard the captured pirogue back to Mississippi.

The Kempers had been rescued, just barely, and only by the quick thinking of Reuben. He had saved his brothers.

Now, he plotted to avenge them.

7
ESCAPE AND REIMPRISONMENT

Peter Ellis Bean
1806

Bean had been granted permission to travel to New Mexico. Four days later, he and his companions were arrested and thrown in a cell. After a few days, a Spanish officer entered the cell and explained that one of the nine of them was to be executed for firing on His Majesty's troops. The former comrades in arms rolled two dice. The man with the lowest score would be hanged for the group's transgressions. Being the youngest, Bean rolled last. One of his companions rolled a four. Bean, a five. His former partner was hanged in the morning.[40]

Bean and his companions were ordered to Acapulco. Along the way, the party spent the night in Salamanca, where a young woman with Native blood offered Bean the chance to escape. She had been married to a rich fifty-five-year-old man she did not love and was looking to make her own escape. She had money and haciendas. Her husband was away. The guard could be bribed.

Yet Bean's conscience and common sense would not let him flee. He couldn't bear to think what would become of his companions once his escape was made known. Furthermore, he believed he would finally be formally released once he reached Acapulco. He declined the young lady's offer.

Years later, still a prisoner in Mexico, he wished he had accepted.[41]

Four hundred miles later, the prisoners arrived in Acapulco. The guard in charge of the prison called out Bean's name, and when he stepped forward,

The California Padres and Their Missions, by Charles Saunders (1915). *Library of Congress.*

the adventurer was thrown into a dark cell, seven by three feet, separated from his companions.

For three months, Bean languished in his cramped, isolated cell with only a lizard to keep him company. He managed to bribe a guard for a small knife, but the stone walls were twelve feet thick and there was no hope of escape.

Desperate to be anywhere but his cell, Bean feigned sickness to be taken to the local hospital. And he was—in double chains. When he arrived, his feet were placed in stocks in addition to the two sets of chains. Bean immediately "recovered," but the shock of moving from the closed air of his tiny cell to the open air of a disease-ridden hospital was too much for his system. For the next three weeks, Bean lay in the foreign hospital on the brink of death. The man next to him died. And then two more passed. Chinch bugs constantly harassed him. His daily allotment of food hardly sustained him.

But Bean was determined to survive. When a priest brought him his daily food, Bean questioned why a recovering man received so little. The priest replied he should eat what he had and that he could go to hell if he wanted more. Bean flew into a rage, throwing the bowl at the priest and striking him a vicious blow to the head. He leapt for his water pot to hurl that as well. But he missed, and the effort knocked him back on his plank bed, the chains tearing the flesh from his shins in the process. For his efforts, Bean's head was placed in the stocks.

The next fifteen days were pure agony for Bean. He was unable to move, and his legs burned from his open wounds. The chinches attacked, constantly gnawing at his skin.

After spending more than a month in the hospital, Bean begged to be allowed to return to his claustrophobic cell.

Only he had no intention of returning to his cell.

Bean's shins were still open wounds, so the doctor had the leg chains removed and two fifteen-pound weights attached at his hips. Three hundred yards from the hospital, Bean suggested to his two guards that the three of them stop for a round of beer. They eagerly complied. They even more eagerly agreed to a second round. Bean then asked one of the guards if he would escort him to the garden out back, where he wished to admire the flowers. When he was alone with the guard, Bean drew a small blade he had concealed and held it to the guard's neck, informing him that he would be escaping. He suggested to the guard, sure to face punishment for drinking while his prisoner escaped, that he should come with him. Seeing doubt in the guard's eyes, Bean gave him some money for bread and told him to meet him at the cemetery.

As the guard ran off to his officer, Bean made his way into a forest, cut loose his chains, and stayed hidden that night. The next day, he snuck into town for food and fortuitously ran into an Irish sea captain, who agreed to hide him aboard his boat and aid in his escape. Unfortunately, once Bean was hidden, a disgruntled cook went to the Spanish authorities and told them there was a runaway on board. Soldiers were sent, and the captain was forced to reveal Bean's whereabouts.[42]

Portrait of a young Texas pioneer, by George Catlin (1830). *Smithsonian American Art Museum.*

Once again, Bean was chained in his old cell, his pet lizard his only company. Aside from his jailer, a priest, his lizard, the workers in the hospital, and an unseen woman who, as she passed below his window, he paid to smuggle a cow's udder full of alcohol to him via a "fishing line" made from the straw of his mat, Bean had no contact with humanity for a year and four months. And then one day, his jailer, while checking his chains, made a stray comment: he was lacking men who understood how to light the charges to blast some rocks. Bean mentioned that he knew how to dismantle rocks. Days later, the sergeant returned and told Bean he was sending him to work at a quarry, but Bean had to promise he would not attempt to run away. Later, Bean wrote, "[B]ut I was determined not to lose an opportunity to escape, if possible: for I was constantly thinking of the chance I had lost at Salamanca, when the lady offered to free me. As soon as the sergeant told me this, I was sure I would escape, or be shot, for I was resolved to risk my life on it the very first chance."[43]

8
OCCUPATIONAL HAZARDS

EDWARD PAKENHAM
1803-1809

The war with Napoleon had become a colonial world war. The sugar islands of the Caribbean were among the chief prizes. So valuable were the French islands and so successful had Napoleon been in Europe that he began to foment designs for an American empire to complement what he had already conquered in Europe. But when the Haitian Revolution drained his coffers and then an entire army, and when resistance in Europe began to stiffen, the French Emperor sold off his continental North American possessions to President Thomas Jefferson. The sugar islands, however, remained his. He needed them; they were too valuable.

Consequently, the British army became determined to seize the valuable islands. Over the next seven years, Britain and its allies captured every French colony in the Caribbean.[44]

JUNE 22, 1803

A small British fleet sailed into the port at St. Lucia on June 21, 1803. Just before five o'clock that evening, British troops disembarked and, within half an hour, captured the French outposts and town of Castries. Only the French fortress on Morne Fortuné stood between Britain and total control of the island. At four o'clock in the morning, Lieutenant-Colonel Pakenham's unit stormed the fort. Shortly after, the fortress surrendered.

At the cost of one day's time, 20 dead, and 110 wounded, Britain captured the valuable Windward Islands. One of those wounded was Lieutenant-Colonel Edward Pakenham, who was shot through the neck. A French family found the wounded officer and brought him to their home, where they cared for him until the British army retrieved him. (Pakenham had prevented his soldiers from harming French civilians in an earlier battle, hence the generous treatment he received at the hands of his enemies.) One month later, Pakenham wrote to his mother from Barbados that he was well and recovering nicely.[45]

February 1, 1809

A twenty-nine-ship, ten-thousand-man British force landed on Martinique with the intent of wrestling the island from the French. The British quickly closed in on the island's capital and its protective fortress. Pakenham's unit stormed the mountain fortress in the face of stiff French resistance. In a turn that was eerily reminiscent of Pakenham's last Caribbean battle six years ago, he was again shot through the neck and shoulders during the assault. Again, he was incapacitated amid victory. Shortly after, Pakenham wrote home to his mother: "The shot passed from the right to the left shoulder, quite at the lower part of the neck! It took leave of me within a hair's breadth of the last. Nearly satisfied with self, delighted with my comrades and proud of my leader, Prevost, I am hourly mending."[46]

Two times now, Pakenham had walked off a battlefield wounded. Two of his brothers were not so lucky.

William Pakenham, captain of HMS *Saldanha*, had gone down in a storm on December 4, 1811. All 253 passengers aboard were lost at sea. (Roughly 200 of the bodies washed ashore on Ireland's west coast. The following August, twenty miles away, a local shot a parrot that was carrying the following inscription on its collar: "Captain Pakenham of His Majesty's Ship Saldanha.")[47] Four months later, Pakenham's brother Hercules was severely wounded while fighting Napoleon's troops in Badajoz, Spain. Hercules survived the wound, but the precariousness of his situation was another reminder of the fragile life of a soldier.

9

BACK TO ACAPULCO

PETER ELLIS BEAN
1807-1808

Within days of his work at the quarry, Bean proposed a plan to his fellow prisoners, both American and Spanish. There were only twenty guards and forty of them. Bean proposed each of them—at a prearranged signal—charge the nearest soldier and wrest his musket from him. The signal would be Bean himself carrying a load of rocks to a guard.

Many agreed to Bean's proposal. The next day, Bean approached a guard, set down his basket, and asked for a light. The guard acquiesced and was soon knocked out, lying on the ground, the victim of a rock to the skull.

Only two of Bean's accomplices fulfilled their end of the plot. The rest fled—but so did the guards. Bean and his army of three now possessed three guns and a bunch of rocks.

Then Bean saw Spanish reinforcements emerge from the town. An elderly companion of Bean's rallied to his side with a basketful of rocks. Bean told his companion to flee; his stones were useless. The prisoner ran off. Bean exchanged three more rounds with his pursuers, but when a contingent of twenty-five approached, he turned and fled. After only fifty yards, he ran into his aged companion again; he was bringing more stones to the fight.

Bean said it was too late; it was time to flee. But the soldiers had closed in. Bean fired his gun. His comrade threw stones. He threw stones until he was shot through the thigh. The potential escapee begged Bean, "My thigh is broke—make your escape; but, before you go, shoot me, for I would rather be shot than taken."[48]

A nineteenth-century depiction of a soldado de cuera, or leather soldier. These soldiers protected New Spain, or Mexico, in the 1700s. *Wikimedia Commons.*

Unable to shoot the man who had stood beside him, facing soldiers with stones alone, Bean made his own escape through a hail of bullets.

Later that day, he joined up with the only other prisoner he could locate. After several days on the run, creeping through woods, slogging through swamps, fleeing locals who had been warned of the escapees, Bean and his companion were surrounded by thirty men. They resisted—futilely. Both were knocked out and chained. The following morning, a contingent arrived to take the duo back to Acapulco. For the third time, Bean was incarcerated in the same castle.

As Bean had escaped before, the governor tried a new stratagem. He chained a large mixed-race man and Bean together, promising the former that he would shave a year off his sentence if he kept a careful eye on Bean. Should Bean cause any problems, the man was free to beat him.

Within three days, Bean was back in his cell, alone. He had beaten the large mixed-race man with a bull skull he'd found in the prison yard. Now, he sat in solitary confinement, this time with two sets of chains anchoring him to the wall.[49]

10

ACROSS THE BORDER

Reuben Kemper
September 23, 1808

Reuben and his brothers, Nathan and Presley, along with supporters, crossed the border into Spanish Territory. That night, their target was Ira Kneeland, the surveyor and adjudicator who had first ruled Reuben's land forfeit and later participated in his kidnapping.

A mile from Kneeland's house, the Kempers veered off into the woods. Two friends rode forward to act as lookouts. A sixth member of the party rode to Kneeland's house and knocked on the door. The surveyor answered and learned that his visitor's friend had fallen deathly ill and needed someone to write out his will. A neighbor had recommended Kneeland. Kneeland agreed, and the pair rode off to record the last testament of the fictious traveler.

A mile later, the Kemper brothers emerged from the woods with pistols drawn. As they stepped into the moonlight, Kneeland's heart stopped, and his stomach dropped. He recognized the scarred Reuben and Nathan. The brothers gagged him, placed a sack over his head, and rode him deep into the woods.

The trio stripped the terrified Kneeland of all his clothes and tied his hands to two trees. All three pulled out whips. The first blow fell on Kneeland's naked back. Then the next. And the next. Reuben landed his whip on Kneeland's shoulders. Nathan thrashed his ribs. Presley, his back. Over and over, the whips cracked and tore the skin from Kneeland's bleeding back. The lashing continued for half an hour without respite.

The Magnolia Mound plantation house in Baton Rouge, Louisiana, is an example of Creole architecture. The house was built in the 1790s. *Library of Congress.*

At last, the brothers dropped their whips. But there was no lull in the torment. Three pairs of fists proceeded to pummel the battered prisoner, turning his skin and muscle to pulp. Reuben then drew his knife as his brothers held Kneeland's head. He proceeded to brand the surveyor by cutting a slice out of each of his ears.

Finally, the torture ended, and the brothers cut the ropes securing Kneeland's hands. Kneeland immediately collapsed in a gory heap. Reuben and his brothers rode off, promising similar treatment to any who aided the Spaniards.[50]

11

ARRIVAL IN NEW ORLEANS

Arsène Lacarrière-Latour
1806–1810

Latour spent the next two years trying to land lucrative contracts in Louisiana and New York. Finally, in 1806, he was back in the Old Southwest, this time in Spanish West Florida, where he received a contract to design a new town that was to be built around the fort at Baton Rouge.

The contract was a major coup for Latour, as it showed not only his skill as an architect/engineer but also the connections he had established after such a brief stay on the American continent. Latour labored over his designs for the next three years, and eventually, the Spanish Governor Carlos de Grand Pré approved his plans. Latour's success in Baton Rouge enabled him to move to New Orleans, where he opened his own architecture firm.

Latour arrived in the Crescent City amid yet another cultural upheaval. New Orleans had been a frequently traded pawn in Europe's never-ending colonial chess match. Constantly being traded to and sacrificed by Spanish and French regimes, the city was now under the control of a new republic: the United States of America.

But new ownership and new freedoms did not necessarily sit well with the entrenched Creole population. In fact, the old-guard Europeans looked down on and treated the upstart Americans with disdain.

Whether the rivals' perceptions were accurate or not, the Creoles viewed the Americans as barbarous vandals, exemplified by the Kaintuck boatmen: uncouth, always drinking, always brawling, men whose lives were doomed to be "nasty, brutish, and short."[51] On the other hand, the Americans saw the

Sailing ships on the Mississippi River in front of New Orleans, by Henry Lewis (1850s). *Internet Archive.*

Creoles as Old World dandies, more fond of dancing, feasting, and carousing than making a living. Lyle Saxon explained the situation: "Now with the two contending forces—snobbishness on the part of the Creoles and intolerance on the part of the puritanical Americans—there was immediate discord."[52]

With each passing year, it seemed inevitable that the Americans would win not just economic but also cultural hegemony over New Orleans. But then the revolution on Saint-Domingue produced unexpected results. Twenty-five thousand refugees fled the Black-controlled island; fifteen thousand of the refugees ended up in New Orleans, ten thousand in 1810 alone.[53] Once again, the cultural makeup of New Orleans was radically altered. Once again, New Orleans reverted to a cultural orbit of the Caribbean.

And the British authorities intended to magnify and exploit the tensions mounting between the various ethnicities.

A culture war was brewing between the Creoles and Americans. Two societies emerged: one in the Vieux Carre, the other above Canal Street. Meanwhile, third and fourth communities were developing in the shadows of the establishment: the gens de couleur, or free persons of color, and the enslaved.

Great Britain hoped to turn three of these discordant communities into a fifth column. So sure were His Britannic Majesty's advisors that the Creole and Black populations of New Orleans would rise in opposition to the Americans that it was assumed to be a given—and vital role—as the British made their plans to capture the Crescent City.

Arsène Lacarrière-Latour was thrown into the mix of this racial gumbo. Due to his recent success as a civil engineer, he also soon found himself with a prominent role in the defense of New Orleans—all of New Orleans—enslaved, gens de couleur, Creole, and American alike.

12
VINDICATION

Reuben Kemper
September 1810–January 1811

The thrashing of Kneeland was not enough to satisfy Reuben's thirst for revenge. He wanted his land and house back, and he wanted to punish the Spanish along the way. He could do both by freeing the Floridas, West and East, from Spanish rule.[54]

Six years after the Kemper brothers' failed assault on Baton Rouge, the city and fort were finally captured by American filibusters on September 23, 1810. Four months later, the United States sent in troops to occupy the disputed city. But until then, the Republic of West Florida flew its flag—a single white star on a blue background—over Baton Rouge. The new republic hoped to wave that same flag over the Spanish territories to its east as well.

Reuben Kemper had no part in the uprising. He heard about it afterward. He would not miss his next opportunity to punish the Spanish.

Before U.S. annexation, the Republic of West Florida appointed Kemper to bring Mobile into the republic's orbit. Kemper quickly accepted. He was given authority, money, and commissions to bring about the annexation of Mobile. But Kemper had bigger plans. He planned to take *all* Spanish lands, all the way to St. Augustine.

Kemper's plans aligned with his friend Andrew Jackson's vision for the Gulf South. The filibuster explained to his fellow patriot, "I was approached by the Convention of West Florida to attempt a reconciliation of our conventional authoritys [*sic*] among the People of Mobille [*sic*] and its neighboring country. To this end (I done as you yourself under similar circumstances would have done) imbarked [*sic*] with Heart and soul devoted to the prosecution of the work of our infant but beloved Country."[55]

On October 20, 1810, Reuben left Pinckneyville, Mississippi Territory, with the intent of liberating the last of the Spanish Gulf coastal lands. Four days later, he arrived at Fort Stoddert, thirty miles north of his objective: Mobile. His first target was lightly defended and ripe for the picking. Any reinforcements from Pensacola would be delayed, as the capital of West Florida was in the throes of a deadly epidemic. (Kemper's old foe, Ira Kneeland, had succumbed to the deadly fever at the same time Reuben arrived at Fort Stoddert.)

Reuben Kemper presides over an independent West Florida government. This illustration originally appeared in William Horace Brown's *The Glory Seekers* (1906). *Internet Archive.*

Reuben moved quickly to take advantage of Spain's weakness. He wrote to Mobile's Spanish commander, Manuel Perez, to ask that he join forces with the filibusters and help overthrow a tyrant king nearly five thousand miles away. Perez and his soldiers would thereby come down on the right side of history, not to mention the side of the victors, as Spain's demise on the Gulf Coast was only a matter of time. Failure to join Kemper and his filibusters would lead to dire consequences: "If we have to resort to arms, the evil and horrors of war will *be laid to your door*! [Y]our answer will decide the fate of yourself and the destiny of your fellow citizens."[56] Kemper gave Perez a concrete deadline to either join forces or surrender.

Perez ignored the threat and began to prepare for the inevitable.

The authorities in Mobile were in a state of hopeless confusion. Where did its citizens—a motley mix of Spanish, French, and American people—stand? To whom did the officers owe their loyalty? Napoleon? Havana? Spain? The West Florida government? The United States had just dispatched troops from Natchez headed toward Mobile. Were they coming to keep an eye on Kemper or take Mobile by force?

Meanwhile, Kemper's November 25 deadline, in which he promised to raise the flag of rebellion on Spanish soil, approached.

On the day of reckoning, Kemper strode up McCurtin's Bluff, just south of the international border. He renamed the hill Bunker Hill and raised the flag of the West Florida Republic.

Confusion reigned, and chaos threatened. Governor Vicente Folch, having recently arrived and taken charge in Mobile, intimated that Spain would soon hand all West Florida over to the Americans. American authorities along the border had heard similar murmurings. But if Kemper and the seventy filibusters who had joined him at the newly ordained Bunker Hill—or his allies marching and plundering eastward from Pascagoula (and likewise flying the Star of West Florida)—could not be controlled, Spain would be forced to defend its sovereign territory. Worse, it might turn to Great Britain for aid.

At the same time, residents of Mobile made it clear that they would welcome acceptance into the United States, but they wanted nothing to do with Reuben Kemper and his banditti from St. Francisville. It appeared most residents south of the border were prepared to support the diplomatic route rather than align with the filibusters.

And still Kemper inched his way south. By December 1, he was within a couple of miles of Mobile, awaiting reinforcements from St. Francisville. With his own money, he bought an additional three hundred muskets with bayonets, twenty kegs of powder, two thousand pounds of musket balls, and a barrel of flints. With this added to his six artillery pieces, Kemper had enough materiel to take Mobile on his own. All he needed now were the men.[57]

Kemper sent one of his trusted aides, Major William Hargraves, with two dozen men to a spot just north of Mobile. Kemper and his unit would join Hargrave's company with the artillery shortly. While on the way to the rendezvous, Kemper was invited to Fort Stoddert in American territory to view correspondence suggesting Mobile was about to capitulate to the United States. On his arrival at Fort Stoddert, Kemper was promptly arrested and taken into custody.

Two days later, Kemper learned that Hargraves's men had been ambushed by one hundred Spanish soldiers from Mobile during a drunken revelry, and all but ten had been killed or captured.[58]

As soon as Kemper was released, he began recruiting followers to free Hargraves and his captured men, whom Kemper claimed Spain was callously abusing. Along the way, of course, he would liberate Mobile itself from Spanish hands. (He even taunted Federal Judge Harry Toulmin that the Star of the Republic of West Florida would fly above Mobile before the Stars and Stripes did.)[59]

With only thirty men, still loyal to a now-defunct Republic of West Florida government (Reuben was unaware of the recent U.S. annexation of Baton

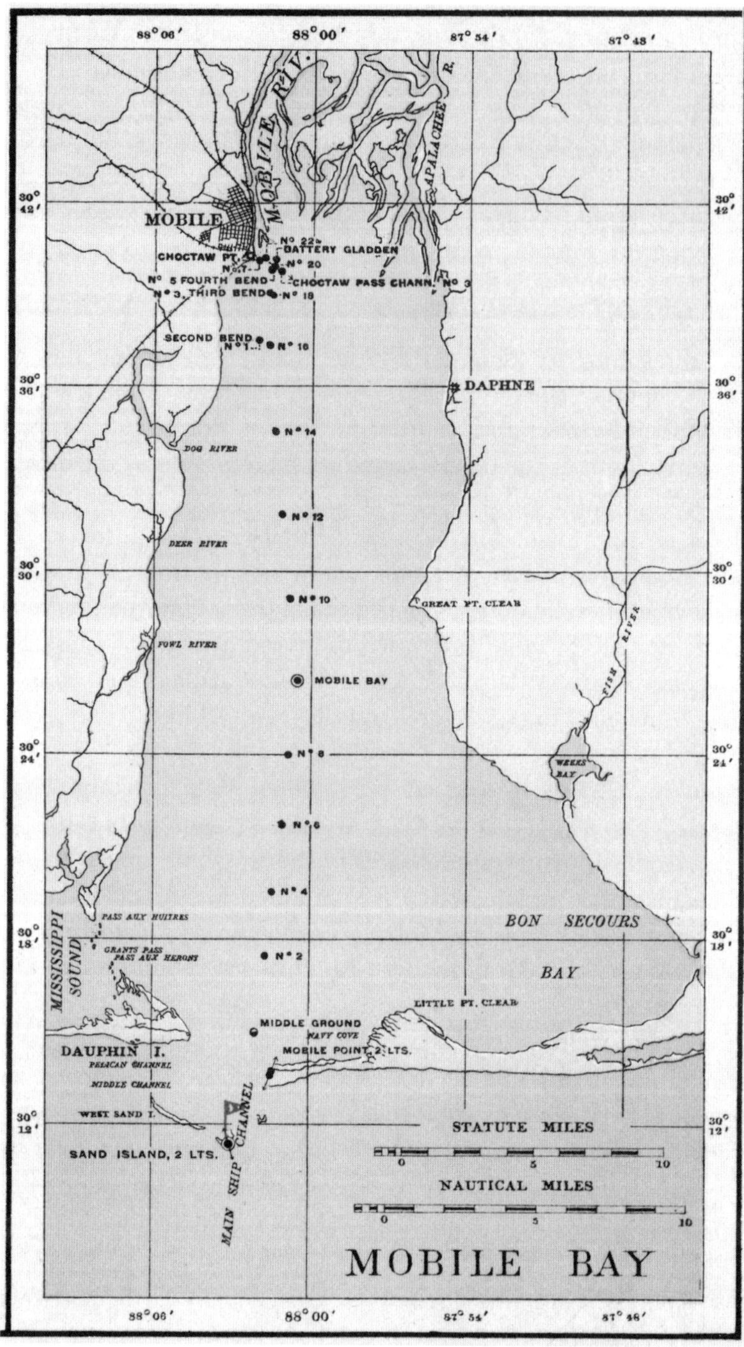

A map of Mobile Bay, showing Mobile Point at the entrance to the bay. *Library of Congress.*

Rouge), Reuben headed toward Mobile. A U.S. force placed itself between Reuben and Mobile. The political situation was a quagmire. Kemper believed Mobile could easily be wrested from the Spanish, but he had no desire to go to war with the United States. Trusting that the United States was determined to take Mobile soon, Kemper returned to a hero's welcome in St. Francisville. Vilified in the eastern press as a filibuster and opportunist, Kemper was fêted at home as a patriot and hero, an inveterate enemy of the Spanish dons.[60]

ULTIMATELY, KEMPER'S ATTEMPT TO take Mobile fell short, but he did contribute to the growing chaos on the Spanish-American border. With British ships prowling the Gulf and Spain seemingly unable to defend itself, President Madison finally authorized American General James Wilkinson to stabilize the region and claim Mobile for the United States.

During March 1813, Wilkinson secretly ordered boats and materiel mobilized to move on Mobile. Gunboats were positioned to intercept any communications with Pensacola. The troops in Fort Stoddert were ordered to be ready to move south and take the bank east of Mobile. Wilkinson led his own forces from New Orleans to Pass Christian.

On April 7, 1813, Wilkinson boarded the sloop *Alligator* and made his move on Mobile. His six hundred troops disembarked at dusk and occupied the woods outside the Spanish city. Wilkinson promptly sent the commandant the same message Kemper had sent him two and a half years before: abandon the city immediately. This time, the Spanish acquiesced, and Mobile finally fell into American hands.[61]

Reuben Kemper's dream of a United States–controlled Gulf Coast was nearly a reality. Andrew Jackson and Washington, D.C. bureaucrats saw that Pensacola, as well as East Florida, would soon be ceded to the United States.

With Baton Rouge and Mobile safely within the American orbit, Reuben Kemper could now turn his attention to the thought that was foremost on his mind: the release of Hargraves and his comrades from the hell known as Morro Prison, Havana, Cuba.

But first, Kemper needed to defend the lands he was instrumental in annexing, for the British were coming.

13

LIFE WITHOUT THE ARMY

EDWARD PAKENHAM
OCTOBER 1811–MAY 1812

Edward Pakenham was a soldier by trade and by choice. At times, wounds caused him to lose, at least temporarily, the camaraderie he had come to rely on. Those times of convalescence showed exactly how much he needed the army.

Having recovered from his wounds, and after seeing brief action in Spain, Pakenham contracted a potentially fatal stomach ailment. He recovered but was sent back to England to continue his recovery. Pakenham stayed with his sister, Kitty, the wife of the Duke of Wellington, who had remained in Spain, intending to liberate Britain's traditional enemy from Napoleon.

Pakenham's four months at home dragged on, as the general was eager to return to his troops. The pain of separation was eased somewhat when he learned he had been promoted to major general. His psychological pain was alleviated even more when he met Annabella Milbanke, a lively and attractive nineteen-year-old heiress to a sizeable fortune. Pakenham was determined to make her his wife. He embarked on a campaign to win Annabella's hand with all the meticulousness he had developed in his martial service to his country. He attempted to woo her with stories of his battles against Napoleon. With tales of Wellington. With yarns of soldiers and cannons and bayonets and charges and all things military.

Annabella found Pakenham boorish. So, when he proposed to her on St. Patrick's Day 1812, her reply was a predictable "no."

Two weeks later, Pakenham was off to Portugal in pursuit of his first love: the army.[62]

(Nearly three years later, Annabella married the notorious poet Lord Byron, who had published *The Corsair*, based on the life of the pirate Jean Lafitte, in 1814. A year after marrying Lord Byron, Annabella gave birth to their only child. A month later, she and her daughter left Byron and moved back to her family. While the Annabella-Byron drama was playing out, Pakenham was involved in his own drama on a plantation outside New Orleans, where he would come to know the Lafitte brothers firsthand.)[63]

Having lost his conquest on the home front, Pakenham was eager to rejoin his army and show his martial spirit on foreign fields. His sister wrote to their brother, Hercules, who was fighting in Spain: "Edward goes to-morrow. I am glad he does, though not as strong as we wish him but he is free from illness and is become so anxious to join you all now that you have been moving, that a longer delay in this country would but vex and irritate his nerves."[64]

By the end of the month, Pakenham was back with his beloved army.

And then he was back in the infirmary, this time with a raging fever. Pakenham did everything in his power to return to the field as soon as possible, but the fever would not abate.

In the meantime, Wellington was putting the finishing touches on his own version of an Iberian Reconquista, slowly driving the French from Portugal and pushing into Spain. In April 1812, Wellington took the strategic city of Badajoz at a tremendous cost. Among the casualties was Pakenham's brother, Hercules. Now, more than ever, Edward Pakenham longed to return to the fields of glory.

14
SALAMANCA

Edward Pakenham
July 22, 1812

The Battle of the Pyramids (1798), Marengo (1800), Austerlitz (1805), Jena-Auerstädt (1806)—Napoleon was steamrolling the European continent. One army after another, one king and then another, one nation and then the next fell to the ambitious Frenchman. At only forty-three, he had already entered the orbits of Alexander and Caesar.

Only a slave insurrection in Saint-Domingue had shown his troops to be vulnerable. But that had occurred nearly a decade ago, on an island 4,500 miles away, with an army he couldn't rush off and save. That loss had led to his sale of New Orleans and all French Louisiana, 828,000 square miles, to the United States at five cents an acre. His dreams of an American empire on hold, Napoleon finally united all of continental Europe. At the same time, he had to hold what he had already conquered.

June 1812 set in motion events that would forever change Western history. Napoleon invaded Russia. The United States declared war on Great Britain. And after four years in Portugal, the Duke of Wellington began his liberating march into Spain.

Napoleon had finally shown signs of weakness. The Iberian Peninsula had become a thorn in his side, but Wellington was determined to make the peninsula Napoleon's doom.

Wellington was determined to capitalize on his bloody and costly victory at Badajoz and pushed deeper into Spain. He marched his army 190 miles north to confront Napoleon's Army of Portugal under the command of Marshal Auguste de Marmont. Each army numbered fifty thousand, of

Napoleon Bonaparte (date unknown). *National Museum of American History.*

which Pakenham was in charge of a division of nearly six thousand. It was a weighty assignment—one he had waited for his entire life.

After days of each trying to outmaneuver the other, the two commanders finally met on July 22, 1812. In an attempt to flank the British, Marmont overextended his own line. Seeing the Frenchman's mistake, Wellington immediately rode to his own flank, where Pakenham commanded and ordered his brother-in-law to attack. As Pakenham rode off, Wellington proudly turned to his staff and exclaimed, "Did you ever see a man who understood so clearly what he has to do?"[65]

Pakenham rewarded Wellington's trust. He marched his men swiftly through a ravine, outflanked the French, and drew his men up in a line of battle before the enemy was aware of his maneuver. Pakenham ordered his men from column to line and rode, hat in hand, to each battalion, giving them encouragement. His cannons, strategically placed on a ridge behind, opened a murderous fire on the French flank. The French guns remained silent, for Pakenham's quick, decisive march had left them no time to deploy. Nor could the French retreat with Pakenham's infantry so close on them. All the flanked French general could do was hope to stand and drive back Pakenham's assault until reinforcements arrived. Pakenham dashed such hope when he gave the order to charge. The French battalions were immediately overwhelmed and fled.

On hearing the battle to the west, Wellington ordered his own units to attack the rest of Marmont's army. With his flank turned and fleeing in confusion, Marmont knew he was doomed. Both he and his second-in-command were shot down. Nearly a third of his army lay dead or wounded on the battlefield. Another third had simply vanished. After the battle, Wellington reported, "I put Pakenham in the 3^d^ Division by General Picton's desire when he was ill, and I am very glad I did so as I must say he made the manoeuvre which led to our success."[66]

The Battle of Salamanca proved a turning point in the war. Coupled with Napoleon's disaster in Russia, Pakenham's actions at Salamanca sealed the emperor's fate. In less than two years, the French conqueror would be sent to Elba in exile. That December, the hero of Salamanca was sent on his own wintry mission to conquer a frigid and swampy land. Pakenham would soon experience the same angst Napoleon had when he stared at a harsh landscape defended by a determined people—so determined, in fact, that they burned their own cities at his advance, something the American general across the lines would threaten to do to New Orleans should Pakenham be victorious.[67]

15

SMUGGLERS

The Brothers Laffite
November 16, 1812–October 1813

November 16, 1812
Little Lake Barataria

Pierre joined his brother, Jean, in the swamps for a routine smuggling mission. The brothers were in Barataria to see one of their privateers set sail on its inaugural voyage. Meanwhile, another privateer landed at the Laffites' base and unloaded its cargo: "twenty-six bales of cinnamon, fifty-four linen shirts, three pieces of Russian sheeting for making bed linen, seven pieces of canvas, one bundle of twine, and one handkerchief."[68] The brothers loaded the goods on five pirogues and began to make their way to New Orleans via the backwaters they knew so well.

As they neared the Rigolets, unmarked boats spotted them and gave chase. The Laffites whipped their pirogues around and made for the opposite shore. The unidentified boats pursued. When they closed to eighty yards, the Laffites demanded to know who pursued them. "United States troops," came the terrifying reply. The smugglers began tossing their contraband overboard, even as they promised to "fire into them & kill them every one" should the pursuit continue. It did. The brothers' crew paddled as frantically as they could and reached the other shore—so did the uniformed troops. As they disembarked, the Laffites again swore to "put every man to instant death" if they came inland.

(397)

Opposite: A young man dressed in a double-breasted jacket, vest and breeches, a cravat, and stockings. His accessories include a corsaire (bicorne or two-sided stitch), walking stick, breloque, and flat shoes. From a Paris fashion magazine, *Journal des Dames et des Modes* (1802). *Rijksmuseum.*

Above: Profile of a pirate, from *The Pirates Own Book* (1837). *Internet Archive.*

It was a vain threat, as a second boat carrying government troops landed in a pincer movement. The Laffites were trapped. Some of their men took off into the woods. One group boarded their pirogue and tried to paddle to safety. They were immediately fired on and forced to surrender.

Pierre and Jean, realizing the futility of their position, surrendered. They were taken, along with other prisoners, to the U.S. camp across the lake and searched. The brothers were found with the cinnamon on them. They were also found to have swords and loaded muskets. The evidence was damning. Jean decided to cooperate, admitting that they had bought the contraband from a privateer who was currently sailing the Gulf.

The brothers were brought to New Orleans and handed over to the court. Their contraband was forfeited and given to their captors, yet the Laffites were released. Pierre stayed in New Orleans, but Jean immediately returned to Barataria.

Two months later, Jean and Pierre's privateer returned, bringing with it a captured Spanish brig carrying seventy-seven enslaved people. Jean sold them on the spot, bringing in more than enough money to pay for the privateer. The brothers quickly outfitted their captured brig as a second privateer.

The brothers remained ashore, Pierre in New Orleans and Jean in Barataria, overseeing the beginnings of a fleet, the genesis of a smuggling empire.[69]

OCTOBER 14, 1813

The brothers Laffite failed to appear for their court hearing. They were given a second chance. They declined. Henceforth, it would be the smugglers' life for them.

Pirogues, weighted down with illicit goods, slithered up the bayous. They always stopped just short of New Orleans, unloaded their goods at a predetermined location, and disappeared again, always in the direction of Barataria.

Soon, those same pirogues began unloading similar goods in broad daylight.

Rumor had it the Laffites had brokered a deal with some privateers/pirates on Cat Island. Contraband was flowing into New Orleans. Most New Orleanians were thrilled. The more ships captured and goods sold to the Laffites, the cheaper the prices in the Crescent City. In effect, the Baratarians were heroes to many.

The U.S. government was no such fan. Washington, D.C., began receiving reports of the Laffites' activity. Customs Inspector Walker Gilbert reported:

> *It is astonishing to what length this piratical business is carried on. It would seem truly to confirm the opinion that we were free; yes free to commit the most heinous crimes with impunity. I saw a person lately from there who informed me that they have regular auctions and from eighty to one hundred persons from New Orleans attend them regularly.*[70]

Walker Gilbert was given the authority to confiscate smuggled goods and arrest any smuggler he could. He soon began seizing stashed goods along the coastline and hunting pirogues that belonged to the Laffite operation. He was beginning to make a small dent in the Laffites' profits. After Gilbert carried out another successful raid on Jean's booty, Jean warned him not to try to take the seizure to New Orleans. But Gilbert would not be swayed from his duties.

On October 12, Jean learned that the customs inspector was cordelling[71] his—the Laffites'—confiscated goods downstream. Jean waited in ambush. Three of his men sailed along Gilbert's keelboat and boarded. Three shots were exchanged in close quarters, and then Jean and his remaining men leapt aboard from the shore. Gilbert promptly surrendered. Seeing one of Gilbert's men wounded, Jean went ashore and found a doctor. He then left Gilbert and his crew at a neighboring house and made off with his re-confiscated goods.[72]

Within two weeks, a list containing the names of anyone who aided the revenue collector was passing through the environs of New Orleans. Should such aid continue, the abettors would lose their lives.

When Gilbert next noticed several pirogues openly and defiantly carrying contraband up Bayou Lafourche, no one volunteered to help him confiscate it.[73]

OCTOBER 1813

Pierre and eighty smugglers paddled their six pirogues up Bayou St. Denis. Suddenly, a longboat appeared in their path. Pierre fired a shot in the air and claimed to be a French unit sailing under French letters of marque. The longboat continued to approach. Pierre ordered his men to fire. Finally, a voice carried across the water, claiming to be a U.S. inspector searching the shore for contraband. Pierre's men fired again and so did the approaching boat. This time, three of Pierre's adversaries fell, wounded. The other captain then identified himself as Captain Amelerq, and he said his longboat carried United States soldiers.

Pierre then swore that he never would have fired on U.S. soldiers if he had known. He offered to take the wounded ashore to a physician but warned he would rather die than lose his cargo.

Captain Amelerq wisely allowed the smuggler to pass unmolested.[74]

The pirate Jean Lafitte plundering the merchant ship *Indiaman*, from *The Pirates Own Book* (1837). *Internet Archive.*

16

"HARDENED TO HICKORY"

ANDREW JACKSON
JANUARY–APRIL 1813

The Battle of New Orleans made Andrew Jackson a national hero.[75] An abortive and futile trip down the Natchez Trace forged a legend.

When war broke out with Great Britain in 1812, Andrew Jackson leapt at the chance for revenge. He hoped for a chance to even his personal score along the Canadian border, where the fighting was heaviest. If such a commission were infeasible, he desired an opportunity to wrest St. Augustine and East Florida from the Spanish. As a last resort, he would accept the consolation of capturing either Mobile or Pensacola.

The third option proved his only hope at military glory, with one corpulent obstacle: General James Wilkinson.

Jackson despised James Wilkinson.

While Jackson was fighting the Redcoats in the Carolinas, Wilkinson was plotting the overthrow of George Washington as a member of the infamous Conway Cabal. Wilkinson survived the backlash and, despite his checkered past, continued to rise in the nascent U.S. Army. In 1812, he was a major general in the U.S. Army and in charge of the United States' Gulf coastal territories, of which New Orleans was his de facto fiefdom. Andrew Jackson was a militia general, subservient to a regular general. Should Jackson end up in the same vicinity as Wilkinson, his troops, his Tennessee Volunteers, would be under the command of Wilkinson. Just in case, Jackson packed his dueling pistols.[76]

Natchez, by Henry Lewis (1850s). *Internet Archive.*

The march down the Natchez Trace was largely uneventful. Cold, dreary, and bored, Jackson's two thousand Volunteers arrived in Washington, six miles from Natchez, when they received word from Wilkinson to stay put. Jackson obeyed and waited. And waited. More than a month later, he was still awaiting orders. Jackson and his men had come to fight, not wait.

March 13, 1813

The rain continued to pour down, seeping through tents, shoes, and clothes. Jackson had 150 men who were noticeably sick, 56 of whom could not walk. Four days prior, he lost a soldier. Today, he lost another—his trumpeter, Benjamin Darnell. Jackson ordered a coffin built. The sawing and nailing echoed throughout his camp. Everyone knew the cause of the commotion.

The rain poured. The hammering continued.

At dusk, the soldier-volunteers assembled. A detachment fired a volley into the air. Benjamin Darnell was placed underground. His comrades trudged back to their camp, wondering who was next.[77]

And then came the ultimate blow: the Tennessee Volunteers were told they were not needed. They were ordered to hand over their equipment to General Wilkinson and return home. They were being asked to make a four-hundred-plus mile return trek through Indian Territory in frigid temperatures with no wagons, tents, or supplies. The sick begged Jackson not to abandon them as their country had.

In his tent, Jackson wrote to his wife, Rachel:

> [I]*t is only by and through me, that these things can be* [done] *the sick shall be taken back as far as lif*[e] *lasts, and supplies shall be had—altho* [sic] *their Patriotism has been but illy rewarded by an ungrateful officer, (not Country) it is therefore my duty to act as a father to the sick and to the well and stay with them untill* [sic] *I march them into Nashville.*[78]

Jackson then made a public oath to his troops. He chose his trusted friend John Coffee to make the address the following morning:

> *The Major Genl having pledged himself that he would never abandon one of his men and that he would act the part of a father to them has to repeat that he will not leave one of the sick nor of the detachment behind. He has led you here. He will lead you back to your country and friends. The sick as far as he has the power and means shall be made comfortable. If any one dies, he will pay to them the last tribute of respect. They shall be buried with all honors of war. Should your General die, he knows it is a respect you will pay to him. It is a debt due to every honest and brave soldier of the detachment.*[79]

The next month proved as harrowing as Jackson feared. He held his men together through pure determination and force of will. Near the beginning of the trek, Jackson dismounted his horse and gave it to an ailing soldier. He would make the rest of the journey on foot, like the majority of his men. Seeing the aged and ailing general walk along like a common private endeared Jackson to his men, and they took to calling him "Old Hickory."

Along the way, Jackson buried more of his Volunteers, more of his comrades. Among them was Thomas Taylor, who finally succumbed to an extended sickness at French Camp. He was buried near the grave of

Andrew Jackson (1896). *Library of Congress.*

Rachel Cravat, the niece of Choctaw Chief Pushmataha.[80]

All along the trek, Jackson feared and anticipated a court-martial upon returning to Nashville. More terrifying, he feared public humiliation as the general who led his troops into a battle he never fought, the general who led his army on a wild goose chase. Instead, Jackson was greeted with ecstatic cheers when he led his bedraggled but unvanquished army into Nashville. The father had returned his sons safely home.

Many of those same sons would march with Jackson again when he made his way to New Orleans six months later.

17

THE DUELIST

ANDREW JACKSON
SEPTEMBER 4, 1813

NASHVILLE

Andrew Jackson was no stranger to the code duello. Before the War of 1812 rolled around, he had been involved in several duels, most of which ended with the duelists either settling beforehand or firing into the air once their courage and honor were verified. (Once, during Jackson's duel with the governor of Tennessee, the governor's horse ran off with his dueling pistols. The two settled their grievances during the interim.)

Not all his duels, however, ended peaceably.

In May 1806, Jackson challenged attorney and noted marksman Charles Dickinson to a duel. The two lined up at twenty-four paces and opened fire. The morning of the duel, Jackson wore an oversized coat to conceal his frame. He waited for Dickinson to fire first, with the intention of taking careful aim himself. Dickinson's ball hit Jackson an inch from his heart. True to his plan, Jackson stood still (witnesses thought Dickinson had missed because of Jackson's stoic posture after receiving the ball to the chest) and took deliberate aim. His own ball pierced Dickinson's abdomen. Within hours, Jackson's adversary was dead.

Dickinson's ball was lodged deep and was too dangerous to remove, so Jackson carried the memento for the rest of his life.[81]

SEVEN YEARS LATER, TWO of Jackson's companions from the Natchez Trace fiasco found themselves embroiled in a bitter argument that quickly degenerated into a duel. Jackson agreed to second one of the participants and arranged the terms of the duel—back to back at ten paces, wheel around and fire on command. Jackson's man emerged victorious when his bullet struck his adversary in the buttocks.

The wounded and humiliated man was the brother of Jackson's aide-de-camp, Thomas Hart Benton, who was in Washington, D.C., at the time, arguing that the government ought to reimburse Jackson for the abortive Natchez Trace campaign. When Benton returned to Tennessee, he blamed Jackson for participating in the duel instead of stopping it. He also accused Jackson of setting rules that clearly worked against the younger Benton. An exchange of letters only escalated the situation. Reminiscent of the deadly exchange between the Montagues and Capulets,[82] Jackson wrote to his former friend asking if the rumors were true that Benton was threatening to challenge him to a duel. Benton denied the rumors but qualified his response by saying he would neither issue nor refuse a duel. He was not frightened of Jackson's pistols. Jackson called Benton a "fish woman" and demanded his old comrade apologize or demand satisfaction. He then swore to friends that the next time he saw the elder Benton, he would horsewhip him.

On September 4, 1813, the Benton brothers, each armed with two pistols, checked into a Nashville hotel. Jackson learned of their presence and, with two similarly armed companions, stormed over to the hotel, horsewhip in hand.

Jackson strode up to Thomas Benton, crying, "Now defend yourself, you damned rascal!" Both men reached for their pistols. Jackson drew first, and a stunned Benton began walking backward into the hotel, Jackson following, pistol aimed at his chest. Unknown to Jackson, the younger Benton had slipped into a door behind him.

Five shots rang out in quick succession—one from the younger Benton, two from the older, and two from Jackson. Only one ball struck its mark. Thomas's shot shattered Jackson's shoulder and lodged in his arm.[83]

Jackson's friends leapt to his defense, and a general melee erupted that included two more misfires, knives, and a sword cane.

With their friend quickly bleeding out, Jackson's comrades left the hotel and brought him to the nearby Nashville Inn. The prognosis was not good. Death was imminent unless Jackson consented to an amputation.

He did not. The physicians tried their utmost, wrapping his arm the best they could. Like the ball in his chest, the one in his arm would remain with him the rest of his days.

Jackson was unable to leave his bed in the Nashville Inn for two weeks. Less than three weeks after receiving his near-mortal wounds, Jackson was ordered to summon the Tennessee militia for a campaign against the Creeks. The next day, Jackson sent out the order, and just thirty-three days after his fight with the Bentons, he was in the saddle, ready to lead his army against the Creeks, the Spanish, the British, anyone his nation—or he—deemed a threat.[84]

18

"FIGHTING NICOLLS"

EDWARD NICOLLS
JULY 1814

Major Edward Nicolls received his newest assignment. He would be heading back to the Americas. Back to the place where he received his first wound. Back to where his legend began.

The thirty-five-year-old Irishman, Protestant, abolitionist, activist, Marine was known throughout the British army as "Fighting Nicolls." His nickname was an understatement. Nicolls had been involved in battles all across the Western Hemisphere. And he had the wounds to prove it. Historian William C. Davis noted, "By 1814 he had suffered a broken left leg and a wounded right, bullets through his body and right arm, a saber cut on his head, and a bayonet thrust in his chest, which combined gave him what a fellow officer described as 'a fantastical deportment.'"[85]

Nicolls enlisted in the Royal Marines at sixteen. He quickly rose in the ranks and began commanding his own ships and detachments. Over the next twenty-four years, he distinguished himself in Saint-Domingue (where his boat, with twelve men, attacked a boat with forty-three men and four cannons; Nicolls killed the other captain but was shot through the stomach in the process), Egypt, Greece, Curaçao, Constantinople, Denmark, and the North Sea, Mediterranean, Atlantic, and Caribbean, all the while accumulating the twenty-four wounds that earned him his sobriquet. By the end of his career, Nicolls had fought in 107 engagements.[86]

Edward Nicolls was also an ardent abolitionist and spent his entire life attempting to end slavery. He despised human bondage, and his new post would give him ample opportunities to fight the injustice.

Nicolls was also a fervent believer in Native rights. Believing that the southern Natives had received a particularly raw deal after the Americans won their freedom, Nicolls vowed to help the abused race win back at least some of their southern lands.

In short, Nicolls's assignment to the Gulf Coast was ideal, as it would enable the Marine major to marry his potent military skills with his idealism.

The eager Marine looked forward to the next chapter in what had already been a legendary career.

19

OF LOVE AND PRISON

THE BROTHERS LAFFITE
JANUARY 20, 1814–JULY 8, 1814

JANUARY 20, 1814

On New Year's Day, Jean distributed fliers around New Orleans proclaiming a slave auction on an island in Barataria; 415 enslaved people would be sold to the highest bidders. The sale was to take place in three weeks. U.S. Customs Inspector John B. Stout was sent to Barataria with a dozen men to stop the Laffite sale. The brothers ambushed the federal agent and killed Stout and two of his men. The brothers then calmly proceeded with their sale. All 415 Black persons were auctioned off that day, while Stout and his two comrades lay in the swamps of Barataria.[87]

Louisiana Governor W.C.C. Claiborne's reaction was swift, and indictments were signed for the Laffite brothers and two of their associates, Renato Beluche and Dominique You.

JULY 8, 1814

Despite the indictment against them, Jean and Pierre continued to travel into New Orleans for business and pleasure. Most times, they came either at night or in disguise. They were wanted by the authorities but needed by the merchants and their customers. So many successful visits into New

Lafitte's alleged blacksmith shop in New Orleans, which was likely built in the 1770s and is considered the oldest building to house a bar in the United States. *Carol Highsmith, Library of Congress.*

Orleans likely made the brothers complacent. Pierre even bought a house in April for his placee, Marie Villard, on Dumaine Street, a house he visited frequently.

Plaçage was a formalized and legal custom common in New Orleans, which allowed for the sexual mixing of the races. A white man would enter negotiations with a mixed-race woman's mother. The object of his desire—her daughter—might be one-half or three-quarters white and either Black or Native. The mother and suitor would arrange terms that would pay a stipend to the mother and provide a house to the placee. The man would also agree to provide furniture and take care of any children that might result from the union. In exchange, the man could visit—or live—in the house whenever he liked, and he would be provided food, coffee, and sex. If the man eventually took a white wife, as often happened, the relationship with the placee would continue if he so desired. If not, he simply notified her that the house and furniture were hers, but the relationship was over.

Pierre and Marie's relationship lasted seventeen years and proved especially fruitful.

In October 1810, Pierre was struck down by a heart attack. This left Pierre periodically paralyzed on his left side, causing fits of trembling. Even his fine penmanship, notable on so many bills of sale, displayed the effects of his condition. The ever-vital Pierre, pirate and lover, was forever hobbled by this health scare.

Hobbled, not humbled. Hobbled, not vanquished. Pierre simply shifted his energies almost exclusively to the business side of the Laffite operations. Jean ran the day-to-day affairs in Barataria and the Gulf.

And Pierre continued his affair with Marie. Their third child was born the year of his stroke. The couple would have four more children together, clear evidence that Pierre's stroke did little to discourage his amorous pursuits.[88]

On July 8, 1814, Pierre was visiting Marie. This time, the authorities learned of the clandestine visit. The U.S. marshal promptly arrested Pierre at his home and dragged him before the court. He was ordered to pay $12,514.52 on the spot. Unable to do so, Pierre was thrown into a narrow, windowless room in the city jail near the Place d'Armes. His legs were placed in shackles, and the outside swing bolt on the door was slammed shut.

Many of the Americans and Spanish of New Orleans were thrilled to read the following day's headline: "Another Emperor Fallen."[89] Governor Manrique of Pensacola wrote to his superior in Cuba, "The infamous and mean Pirate Lafitte has been arrested and jailed for the enormous crimes, offenses and other complaints against him."[90]

The seriousness of Pierre's predicament became clear twelve days later, when a grand jury finally convened and new charges were added "for having knowingly & wittingly aided & assisted, procured, commanded, counselled & advised…acts of piracy & robbery upon the high seas…and for having received & repeatedly introduced goods, wares & merchandise arising from such piratical captures into this District."[91]

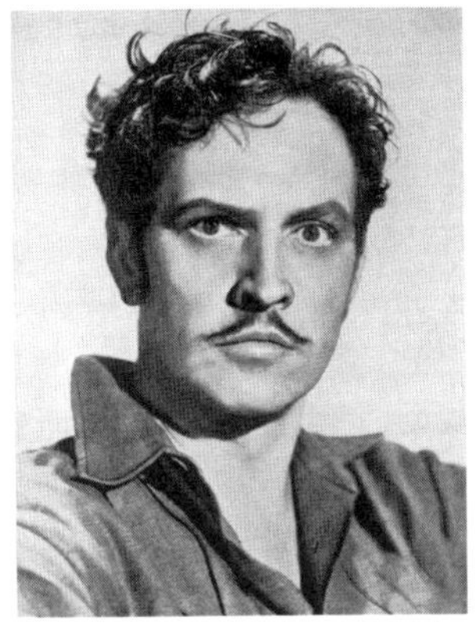

The actor Fredric March portraying Jean Lafitte in Cecil B. DeMille's *The Buccaneer* (1938). *Internet Archive.*

Jean was naturally prepared to pay the original bail, but the new charges—plus the Laffites' penchant for skipping bail—convinced the judge to hold Pierre until he could be convicted. Jean retorted by attempting to have Pierre released on a medical discharge due to his recent heart attack. The prosecution provided their own doctor, who claimed that Pierre's confinement was no detriment to his health, nor were the chains still bound around his feet. All the smuggler needed was some outdoor exercise every now and then.[92]

Pierre would remain in jail until his trial—and probable hanging.

20

APALACHICOLA

EDWARD NICOLLS
JULY–AUGUST 14, 1814

In July 1814, Edward Nicolls brought his military prowess and courage to the Gulf Coast—and his fiery abolitionism. Landing at Apalachicola, Nicolls was tasked with raising an auxiliary army for the New Orleans campaign. His force comprised one hundred British Marines, who served as combatants and mentors, along with disgruntled Natives and runaway enslaved people. Nicolls believed he could also convince disaffected Creoles, most notably the Laffites' Baratarians, to His Majesty's standard.

Despite their defeat at Horseshoe Bend, the unvanquished Creeks promised Admiral Cochrane that they could still field an army of three thousand warriors. If Britain matched that number, the combined force could drive the Americans out of the Gulf region. Cochrane quickly acquiesced and appointed Marine Major Nicolls as the liaison between British and Creek forces.

On arriving at Apalachicola, two hundred miles east of Pensacola, in July, Nicolls began recruiting Native and Black troops. He was armed with a proclamation from Admiral Cochrane that promised freedom and employment to any enslaved American who fled to British lines.

> *WHEREAS, it has been represented to me, that many Persons now resident in the UNITED STATES, have expressed a desire to withdraw therefrom, with a view of entering into His Majesty's Service, or of being received as Free Settlers into some of His Majesty's Colonies.*
>
> *This is therefore to Give Notice,*

Above: Portrait of the Freys, an Anglo-Creole New Orleans family, with their enslaved Afro-Creole laborer Bélizaire (1837). *Metropolitan Museum of Art.*

Opposite: "So, Uncle Tom, where are you going?" *Rijksmuseum.*

> *That all those who may be disposed to emigrate from the UNITED STATES will, with their Families, be received on board His Majesty's Ships or Vessels of War, or at the Military Posts that may be established, upon or near the Coast of the UNITED STATES, when they will have their choice of either entering into His Majesty's Sea or Land Forces, or of being sent as FREE settlers to the British Possessions in North America or the West Indies, where they will meet with due encouragement.*
>
> *Given under my Hand at Bermuda, this 2nd day of April, 1814, ALEXANDER COCHRANE.*[93]

In addition to the proclamation, Nicolls was provided two thousand muskets, two thousand swords, and two cannons, as well as uniforms for his new Black and Native recruits.[94] He immediately established a base and began to build and train his new army.

Nicolls's optimism reached the highest levels of the British command. Based on Nicolls's reports, Cochrane wrote to the secretary of war that because of Nicolls's success in raising a fifth column, he needed only two thousand regulars to take New Orleans. Instead, Cochrane was sent the Chesapeake units, as well as reinforcements from England under General Edward Pakenham. He commanded an army plenty large enough to subdue the Gulf South. To make matters even more promising, Nicolls sent the admiral a note claiming that sources told the Marine major that the Creoles would support the capture of New Orleans.

So far, the only hitch occurred when Nicolls landed in Havana, hoping to ensure Spanish cooperation in Pensacola. When he found out that the Spanish would not allow the British to use Pensacola, Nicolls went to a tavern and began boasting that he just might take Pensacola anyway, and when he did, Black Americans would flock to his coastal standard.[95] Nicolls's imprudent boasts were passed on to Andrew Jackson. The "impatient blustering Irishman" had let Britain's plans slip.[96] Now, Jackson was certain New Orleans was the target.

21
BLADENSBURG AND WASHINGTON, D.C.

George Robert Gleig
August 24, 1814

George Robert Gleig, the son of the Scottish Bishop of Brechin, wanted to do his part to end the Napoleonic menace. He resolved to turn down the scholarship he had been offered to study at Oxford. Though his son was an intelligent man with a promising career in the field of academia, Gleig's father supported George's decision and provided the funds needed to ensure his boy joined the staff of the Duke of Wellington as an ensign.

Nine months later, the Duke of Wellington decisively defeated Napoleon's forces at the Battle of Toulouse between April 10 and 12. On entering the city, Gleig and his commander learned that Napoleon had abdicated four days before the battle. This was not the last costly and bloody battle that Gleig would fight, ignorant that peace had already been negotiated.

With Napoleon in exile, His Britannic Majesty was determined to crush the upstart Americans overseas. He now had the army needed to do so, the same army that had just vanquished Europe's most potent conqueror.

Gleig and his 85th Regiment were promptly sent across the Atlantic as part of a grand new strategy to subdue the King's former subjects—and regain some of the lands formerly lost and perhaps add a port city into which over 40 percent of the United States' rivers flowed.[97]

On August 24, 1814, Gleig marched with his army toward the American capital at Washington, D.C. Five miles outside the capital, they came upon the U.S. Army, which had deployed 6,500 men and 20 cannons in three distinct lines to defend the Anacostia River and the lone bridge into the town of Bladensburg.

G.R. Gleig. *New York Public Library.*

Despite being outnumbered, General Ross gave the order to advance on the bridge. Gleig's 85th Light Infantry, vanquishers of Napoleon, dutifully advanced into the cannons' mouths. The first volley devastated the lead company. Still, the 85th advanced. American muskets added to the death toll. And still, the British came, marching over the bodies of their fallen comrades. Within minutes, they had taken control of the bridge. Soon after, they had control of the opposite bank. The disciplined British quickly scattered the American skirmishers and captured the two cannons covering the bridge. But now, the Americans' second line held firm and even counterattacked. The British were driven back toward the bridge, but when reinforcements arrived, they regrouped. The outcome of the battle was briefly in doubt, as the Americans' second line and British beachhead exchanged volleys. In a standing fight, the discipline of the British won the day. The American units began to break, and soon, a general rout was on.

The American left broke into a run, and the British pounced. Rather than regroup to defend the capital, the American forces scattered in disarray. The Battle of Bladensburg was an unmitigated success for British arms. Even more importantly, the road to Washington, D.C., was now undefended.

The Battle of Bladensburg would have lasting consequences in the War of 1812. Although Gleig's commander, Colonel William Thornton, received a serious wound, the general behavior of the American army reinforced the contempt with which British leadership held the American forces. Gleig would later write:

> *Being in possession of a strong position, they were of course less exposed in defending, than the others in storming it; and had they conducted themselves with coolness and resolution, it is not conceivable how the battle could have*

> *been won.... [N]o troops could behave worse than they did. The skirmishers were driven in as soon as attacked, the first line gave way without offering the slightest resistance, and the left of the main body was broken within half an hour after it was seriously engaged.*[98]

That same dismissiveness would accompany British leadership to New Orleans four months later.

THE SAME AFTERNOON THE British routed the Americans at Bladensburg, Ross's troops halted outside the American capital. Ross sent a flag of truce to negotiate the surrender of the city and exact a ransom. Gleig related what happened next:

> *But whatever his proposal might have been, it was not so much as heard; for scarcely had the party bearing the flag entered the street, when it was fired upon from the windows of one of the houses, and the horse of the General himself, who accompanied it, killed. The indignation excited by this act throughout all ranks and classes of men in the army, was such as the nature of the case could not fail to occasion. Every thought of accommodation was instantly laid aside.*[99]

Partly in revenge for the American burning of York, Canada, the previous year and partly to punish the would-be assassins, Gleig and his comrades stormed the capital and began putting public buildings to the torch. The President's Mansion, Capitol, dockyard, arsenal, and barracks all erupted in flame.[100]

York had been avenged, the Americans had been punished, and men like George Robert Gleig were reassured that the Americans would prove far easier foes than Napoleon had been. That night, Gleig gloried in being a British soldier:

> *The sky was brilliantly illumined by the different conflagrations; and a dark red light was thrown upon the road, sufficient to permit each man to view distinctly his comrade's face. Except the burning of St. Sebastian's I do not recollect to have witnessed at any period of my life a scene more striking or more sublime.*[101]

22
JEAN CHOOSES A SIDE

THE BROTHERS LAFFITE
SEPTEMBER 3, 1814

GRAND TERRE

Boom!

A cannon echoed across the water. Jean Laffite boarded a small boat with four others to ascertain the meaning of the shot. As he approached the bay, he noticed a British sloop waiting between Grand Isle and his Baratarian base on Grand Terre. The sloop flew a white flag, so Laffite ordered his men to approach. An officer introduced himself across the bay as Captain Nicholas Lockyer, and he said he desired to speak with Jean Laffite.

Laffite offered to lead the British officer to "Monsieur Laffite," implying that he was at his house on Grand Terre. The officers followed, and only when they reached the smuggler's house did Laffite introduce himself as the man they sought.

Shocked but not deterred, Lockyer handed Laffite a packet of letters. One document contained a startling offer from the British government: if Laffite and his fellow Baratarians would assist the British in capturing New Orleans, the outlaws would be rewarded handsomely. First, they would receive amnesty for a decade of illegalities. Second, they would receive lands in proportion to their ranks. Third, Laffite himself would be made a captain in His Britannic Majesty's navy. Finally, Laffite was offered $30,000 to help make his decision.

Lockyer returned to his ship and awaited Laffite's answer. It came just a few hours later: "If you could grant me fifteen days to put my affairs in order…I will be entirely at your disposal."[102]

A portrait of Pierre le Turcq, a famous privateer who sailed with John Paul Jones in the late 1700s, by Pieter Willem van Megen (1783). *Rijksmuseum.*

Satisfied that he had secured the support of Jean Laffite and his Baratarians, Lockyer sailed away, fully expecting to be fighting alongside Laffite in two weeks.

Mortified that his smuggling empire was teetering on the edge of collapse, Laffite sat down to write his own letters—letters that would be delivered to American authorities along with the four he had received from Captain Lockyer.

It did not take long for the smuggler to ponder Britain's offer—and it was not as enticing as Lockyer thought. A promise of land to a man of the sea was useless. Laffite was not prepared to lay aside his lucrative business at sea in exchange for the difficult life of a sedentary farmer. As for a captainship in the Royal Navy, Laffite was already a captain. And more than that, he had a growing fleet at his disposal. Why would he willingly submit to the commands of the British navy—known for its stern discipline—with little chance to enrich himself? And $30,000? Laffite could earn that—and far more—privateering and smuggling.

Additionally, British control of the Gulf Coast would certainly put an end to his smuggling empire. British ships were more numerous and more committed to ending piracy and enforcing customs laws than the Americans'. The Laffites would also be required to cease their attacks on all British allies, including Spain. The overwhelming majority of their profits came from taking Spanish ships. The Laffites' letters of marque to attack Spanish shipping from newly independent, revolutionary South American governments would no longer be valid. In fact, such attacks from a British-held Gulf Coast would end in the hangman's noose.

In effect, Laffite's entire world would come crumbling down around him.

It was far better to live under the domain of the largely impotent United States.[103]

Jean immediately sent the British correspondence and offer to his friend and Louisiana legislator Jean Blanque, along with the following note:

> *Our enemies have endeavored to work on me by a motive which few men would have resisted. They have presented to me a brother in irons, a brother who is to me very dear! Whose deliverer I might become, and I declined the proposal. Well persuaded of this* [sic] *innocence, I am free from apprehension as to the issue of a trial; but he is sick and not in a place where he can receive the assistance his state requires. I recommend him to you, in the name of humanity.*[104]

That very night, the door to Pierre's cell mysteriously swung open. The elder Laffite, who had been in prison eight weeks, was now a free man. He immediately made his way to Jean in Barataria.

23

THE NEW ORLEANS STATION

DANIEL TODD PATTERSON
JULY 1813–SEPTEMBER 1814

On March 21, 1808, Daniel Patterson was sent to the New Orleans Station to serve under Captain David Porter. Within two years, he was given a de facto independent command of twelve gunboats stationed between Natchez and the Gulf.

On July 24, 1813, Patterson was appointed master commandant of the New Orleans Station, and he promptly began to prepare the city for an invasion. With a clear understanding of the importance of the Mississippi River and, hence, New Orleans to U.S. interests, Patterson sought to protect all approaches to the important port. However, he very soon realized, "The approaches to this city…by water are so numerous that they require many vessels and vigilant officers to guard them effectively."[105] He planned to use his schooner *Carolina* and sloop *Louisiana* to defend Forts St. Leon and St. Philip along the Mississippi River. He would also use fireships if necessary. The rest of his gunboats would patrol the bayous and bays east of New Orleans. In short, Patterson had too few ships and sailors to effectively defend the city. He was spread too thin, but he believed that no matter which route the British took, he could delay them long enough for the U.S. Army to hasten to the city's defense.[106]

Patterson's commission to the New Orleans Station entailed a joint mission: counter-piracy and the defense of New Orleans. When General Andrew Jackson requested part of Patterson's flotilla to defend Fort Bowyer, the gateway to Mobile, Patterson declined and went after Laffite's Baratarian base instead. On September 16, 1814, as Fort Bowyer stood alone against

A pirate ship destroying a merchant vessel, from *The Pirates Own Book* (1837). *Internet Archive.*

a seemingly overwhelming British force, Patterson landed on Barataria with the 44th U.S. Infantry and some Marines.[107]

Jackson was incensed that Patterson had defied him. Although the master commandant wrote a respectful letter to the general insisting that New Orleans was Britain's true objective and that he needed his limited men and boats closer to the city, Jackson fired off a letter to the secretary of war complaining about Patterson withholding his gunboats. The War Department supported Patterson: there were to be two separate chains of command, Army and Navy.

Patterson and Jackson had reached a turning point in their relationship. Failure to settle their differences and cooperate would likely doom the defense of New Orleans. Military historian Matthew Dale explains the significance of Jackson's ultimate reaction to Patterson's defiance:

> *While the mandate initially presented a personal affront to Jackson, the agreed upon operational employment of Army and Navy forces in the Gulf region, in fact, established the parameters for what became a successful relationship developed between Jackson and Patterson. Jackson possessed no experience with naval operations or technology and thus suffered from a rough learning curve, instead learned as he went from Patterson, who proved a patient teacher.*[108]

Neither Patterson nor Jackson envisioned exactly how close they would be working together over the next four months.

24

THE BATTLE OF BALTIMORE

GEORGE ROBERT GLEIG
SEPTEMBER 12–14, 1814

With Napoleon in exile and Washington, D.C., in ashes, the British continued to pursue an aggressive strategy and turned their attention north toward Baltimore. Whereas Washington, D.C., had been a mostly symbolic victory—the city being a compromise locale that would house the United States government—Baltimore was a thriving port, strategically located on the Mid-Atlantic coastline. The destruction of America's capital *and* Baltimore, the nation's third-largest city and a thriving commercial hub, would give Britain an enormous advantage when it came time to negotiate an end to the war.

So important was Baltimore to Britain's revised strategy for the 1814 campaign that when a three-pronged assault was devised, a full third of the troops under the more than capable General Robert Ross was set aside for the Mid-Atlantic invasion.

The capture of Baltimore was expected to be swift and easy. General Ross would land five thousand troops eight miles outside the city and march overland. Meanwhile, Admiral Alexander Cochrane would bombard and capture Fort McHenry at the foot of the Patapsco River. The combined assault would not only take the vital port city but also further demoralize the Americans and eliminate a popular privateer base that had been harassing British shipping.

GLEIG AND HIS COMRADES were given three days' food and eighty rounds of ammunition.[109] As preparations for the amphibious operation and subsequent attack progressed, Gleig vacillated between activity and reflection. Later, he gave his readers an insight into a soldier's mind before (and during) battle:

> *But no man of the smallest reflection can look forward to the chance of a sudden and violent death without experiencing sensations very different from those which he experiences under any other circumstances. When the battle has fairly begun, I may say with truth that the feelings of those engaged are delightful; because they are in fact so many gamblers playing for the highest stake that can be offered. But the stir and noise of equipping, and then the calmness and stillness of expectation, these are the things which force a man to think.*[110]

The expeditionary force landed on September 12 and began their march toward the port city. Five miles outside of Baltimore, they were confronted by a small force of American skirmishers and marksmen. When the British advance units were fired on, General Ross galloped to the front to ascertain the situation. Not long after, Gleig saw an aide-de-camp hastening to the main body and calling for a surgeon. Gleig's heart sank, and his worst fear came to fruition when he saw Ross's riderless and bloodstained horse hurtling from the front. Moments later, Gleig marched by General Ross laid out beside the road. The general had just asked that his family be provided for. Soon after, he was carried toward the fleet but died along the way.[111]

As happened at Bladensburg, disciplined British troops carried the day, and the Americans were forced to retreat. Yet this time, the Americans stood longer and withdrew in greater order. Their delaying action slowed the British advance and gave their own general more time to prepare his defenses in Baltimore.

The Americans were toughening.

And Great Britain had lost one of its most successful generals.

AFTER THE BRITISH REGROUPED outside Baltimore, Ross's replacement decided to take the port city itself. However, after reconnoitering, he discovered the defenses were too strong. He needed Admiral Cochrane to first reduce Fort McHenry.

After more than twenty-four hours of bombardment, Fort McHenry still stood, relatively unscathed. As Francis Scott Key proudly watched the "star-spangled banner yet wave, o'er the land of the free and the home of the brave," Cochrane's fleet withdrew to sea.

Gleig and his comrades soon joined the sailors as British plans were forced to evolve.

A MONTH EARLIER, GLEIG had reflected, "In America, every man is a marksman from his very boyhood, and every man serves in the militia; but to bring an army of raw militiamen, however excellent they might be as marksmen, into a fair field against regular troops, could end in nothing but defeat."[112] On September 12, his prophecy was fulfilled—but at a tremendous cost. His Majesty was now forced to scour his ranks for a replacement to lead his forces across the pond.

His first choice was the Duke of Wellington.

He would be forced to accept his second option: the Iron Duke's brother-in-law.

Soon, George Robert Gleig, now on his way to Port Royal, Jamaica, would find himself under a new commander. In just a few months, he would find himself once again confronted by an entrenched and determined foe. The outcome of his next battle would be far bloodier and more climactic.

25
FORT BOWYER

EDWARD NICOLLS
SEPTEMBER 14, 1814

After the Red Stick Creeks' disastrous defeat at Horseshoe Bend, Edward Nicolls needed a victory to impress his Native allies. Many had fled to the Spanish Floridas. Nicolls believed that only a victory over the Americans would bring the Natives back to British ranks.

The British high command had already devised a plan to crush the Americans. As an added benefit, the presently disillusioned Natives would recognize the weakness of the Americans and flock back to the British standard, reclaiming their recently lost lands and forming a formidable buffer between Britian and the United States.

His Majesty's forces would take Mobile, thereby cutting off New Orleans's trade with the east. The expeditionary force would then take Natchez, cutting off aid and reinforcements via the Mississippi River. New Orleans would be isolated and inevitably fall into British hands with minimal loss of life.

Only dilapidated Fort Bowyer and 160 men of the U.S. 2nd Infantry under Major William Lawrence stood in their way.[113]

Nicolls saw the wisdom in approaching New Orleans from Mobile. He and Captain William Percy worked together to develop the battle plan that would take Fort Bowyer and set the campaign in motion. Nicolls would land 60 Marines and 180 Native allies nine miles east of the fort on September 12, 1814. At the same time, Percy would sail his squadron of 4 sloops carrying 78 cannons within range of the stronghold. Nicolls was assured the mission would be easy and that the sloops would get to within pistol shot of the fort.

However, just before the attack, Nicolls fell ill and was forced to hand the land command over to Marine Captain Robert Henry. And then the battle proceeded as planned—that is until everything began to go awry for the British forces.

As Nicolls eagerly awaited news of his outfit, Captain Henry marched them quietly to within eight hundred yards of the fort. Convinced that he had maintained the element of surprise, he ordered his howitzer brought forward and prepared his men to top the dune and storm the last half mile of beach to take the fort.

It was a rash decision. The fortified Americans fired back, and Henry quickly realized he could not take the fort alone. Instead, he decided to postpone the attack and act in concert with the Royal Navy, when most American men and guns would be directed seaward instead. And when the Americans inevitably retreated, he would be in position to finish them off.

Later that day, Captain Percy moved in as planned. Soon, Fort Bowyer would either be in ashes or beneath a British flag, its garrison prisoners.

As promised, Percy sailed directly under the American guns and unleashed a barrage at the dilapidated fort. Almost simultaneously, Henry's Marines and Natives charged the fort. They were immediately repelled. They would

Mobile Bay in 1841, by William Todd. *New York Public Library.*

spend the rest of the battle behind their sand dune, awaiting an American retreat that never materialized.[114]

Percy's squadron, with Nicolls aboard, moved on the fort at 3:00 p.m. The first two ships, the *Hermes* and *Sophie*, were firing by 4:30 p.m. But then the wind stopped. The other two British ships were unable to join the fray. Worse, the fire from the *Hermes* and *Sophia* was proving ineffective, largely because the cannons had to be raised to the maximum height to hit the fort. Fort Bowyer, on the other hand, profited greatly from the stagnant wind, especially after the *Hermes*'s bow spring was hit and the ship drifted aimlessly in the bay, a sitting duck for Bowyer's guns.

An ill Nicolls could not resist defending the ship. Shot after shot pounded the *Hermes*, and still, Percy and Nicolls tried to save the ship. Nicolls received two additional wounds, the most serious being the permanent loss of his right eye. By early evening, it was clear that the battle was over and the *Hermes* doomed. Percy evacuated the wounded and set fire to the largest frigate in his squadron.[115]

The poorly coordinated assault of Fort Bowyer cost the British twenty-four dead and forty-four wounded—and, of course, the *Hermes*. More importantly, the British strategy of taking Mobile and advancing on New Orleans overland was shelved in favor of a far more dangerous amphibious assault.[116]

26

BARATARIA

Daniel Todd Patterson
September 16, 1814

Master Commandant Patterson had had his fill of pirates. After two years in a pirate prison six thousand miles away from his home country, Patterson was in no mood to tolerate pirates in his homeland.

On September 15, 1814, Patterson took the schooners *Carolina* and *Seahorse*, along with six gunboats and three barges, into the swamps south of New Orleans. He was determined to drive the Laffites and their band of "hellish banditti" from the swamps of Barataria.[117]

Laffite, meanwhile, had gotten wind of Patterson's expedition. However, he had already planned a massive sale on September 16. He gambled that he could move his goods and make his escape before Patterson's fleet arrived.

It was a near-fatal miscalculation.

Patterson's flotilla arrived at 8:30 a.m.—sooner than Laffite expected. At 10:00 a.m., Patterson's ships advanced in battle formation. Laffite had allowed each captain to make his own decision regarding the American threat. It was every man for himself. Many buyers and smugglers leapt into small boats and raced for the shore. A handful of privateers from Cartagena were determined to give battle. Others surrendered. Some set flame to their ships. It was a scene of utter chaos. Within two hours, Patterson had captured the entire "Baratarian fleet." Among the captured was the Laffites' most trusted aide, Dominique You.

Patterson ordered his men ashore where they began to gather the smugglers' loot. They ransacked the island of anything valuable and then set fire to its forty houses and warehouses. They also set the watchtower and

Fort Livingston on the Gulf of Mexico, Barataria, Louisiana (1853). *New York Public Library.*

small and damaged craft aflame. Patterson ordered the valuable boats to fall in line with the intent of auctioning them off in New Orleans.

With the Laffite base burning behind him, the Baratarian operation shattered, and the smugglers either captured or scattered shipless in the swamps,[118] Patterson hauled his catch to New Orleans, where he was amply rewarded. His dismantling of Barataria had demonstrated his competency as a commander and brought back to the city an astounding $250,000 worth of goods and ships.[119]

27
THE APPOINTMENT

EDWARD PAKENHAM
OCTOBER 1814

Edward Pakenham was not the administration's first choice to command His Majesty's forces in America. That honor had previously belonged to General Robert Ross. But when Ross was killed outside Baltimore by an American marksman, Britain began looking for a replacement. The honor naturally fell to the victorious Duke of Wellington. Wellington, however, believed that Britain's second war with its former colonies would end the way the first one had. Thus, there was little glory to be won on the other side of the Atlantic. Wellington politely declined the honor.

Pakenham was the next logical choice. He had been a competent assistant to the duke, and after his heroics at Salamanca, he had a name that inspired confidence. Hence, the ministry requested that Pakenham become the chief commander of the southern operation.

Like his brother-in-law, Pakenham was wary of the offer. On receiving his commission, he wrote to his mother:

> *It was my expectation when I left you to have returned to our little party at the Lodge. Public Events have otherwise determined my private moments. The Affairs in America have gone ill. Staff officers have become necessary, and I have been called on by the Ministers to proceed to the other side of the Atlantic. I confess to you that there is nothing that makes this employment desirable.*[120]

Nevertheless, he felt duty bound to accept the commission and began making preparations to sail to Jamaica.

Because Pakenham was to arrive late on the scene, his initial role would be as a tactical field commander. The general strategy had already been determined on a macro and micro level.

The grand strategy had been a three-pronged assault, one from Canada, another in the middle colonies, and a third in the Gulf. Aside from the largely symbolic burning of Washington, D.C., the first two phases had failed. With negotiations to end the war ongoing in Ghent, it was imperative that Britain seize the initiative and claim some territory to use as a negotiating chip. It was up to General Pakenham to present Britain's negotiators with that chip.

On the more parochial strategic level, Admiral Alexander Cochrane devised the plan Pakenham would be forced to follow.

Ironically, Pakenham and Cochrane had worked together at the Battle of Martinique five years prior, when Pakenham received his second neck wound. Cochrane was a seasoned naval officer who was both decorated and arrogant. Though respected, Cochrane tended to dominate a discussion and force his will on others. When he was surrounded by younger, subservient officers, his disposition limited discussion and often silenced other points of view. Cochrane's abrasiveness, along with the interim commander's reluctance to defy him, would have disastrous effects on the Gulf campaign.

The plan Pakenham inherited focused on the capture of New Orleans.

Admiral Cochrane initially sought to foment a Native war and take Mobile in the process. He would then use his base and Native auxiliaries and march over land on New Orleans.

Andrew Jackson had spoiled both plans. The Battle of Horseshoe Bend (concomitant with the late arrival of British arms) had scattered the Red Stick Creeks. His decision to keep the bulk of his troops in Mobile made an assault on that city impractical.

The initial plan called for an Admiral Cochrane–General Ross rendezvous in Negril, Jamaica. Ross's death left the British administration scrambling to find a replacement. Pakenham was ultimately sent. The journey from London to Jamaica was three thousand miles longer than the trip from Baltimore to Jamaica. Inevitably, Pakenham would be late.

New Orleans, however, sat mostly undefended. With Jackson in Mobile and a large British reinforcement on the way, Cochrane decided New Orleans was ripe for the taking. With Pakenham still crossing the Atlantic, the admiral hoisted sails for the Crescent City.[121]

Pakenham arrived two days after *his* army had already landed, fought, and been pinned down with entrenched American troops to the front, the waters of Lake Borgne behind.

For the next two weeks, Pakenham would vacillate between Charybdis and Scylla, between withdrawal and assault, between Cochrane and himself.

28
PENSACOLA

Andrew Jackson
November 7–9, 1814

Andrew Jackson hated the British. Spain was allied with Great Britain. By extension, he hated Spain.

Fortunately, the Spanish Floridas were weak and waning. By contrast, the United States was waxing and expanding. Pensacola would be an easy conquest. Jackson's problem? The United States and Spain were at peace.

And yet Jackson was certain that Spain was working against U.S. interests. It was no secret that Spanish policy revolved around using the Native tribes as a buffer to U.S. encroachment. The Creek, Choctaw, and Chickasaw tribes, armed and under the patronage of Spain, served as a deterrent to American expansion. After the massacre at Fort Mims on August 30, 1813, an event that galvanized Americans like none other since the Battle of Lexington, it was discovered that Spain had provided the gunpowder that enabled the Red Stick Creeks to put to death 250 Americans and their Creek allies. Even worse for Spain, American forces later captured a letter from the Spanish governor of West Florida congratulating the Creeks on their bloody victory and promising further Spanish aid in the fight against the United States.[122]

Just as threatening to U.S. security was Spain's willingness to disregard fugitives who escaped slavery after crossing into the more lax/incompetent Spanish Floridas. An easily accessible safe space for runaways so close to the southern border—where most enslaved Americans resided—was problematic. A growing maroon colony of Black fugitives adjacent to a land where the enslaved often outnumbered white residents was a national security threat. Since the invention of the cotton gin, the greatest fear of white southerners was a massive slave rebellion. In Jackson's mind, a colony of free Black people just south of the border was a threat to the institution of slavery itself.

But what irked Jackson the most was Spain's recent cooperation with Britain. Although Spain was officially neutral, the governor of Spanish West Florida, Mateo González Manrique, had allowed Britain to disembark agents and supplies intended for the Natives in Spanish Territory. These weapons and materiel made their way into hostile hands. Furthermore, British soldiers and Marines, such as Edward Nicolls, were actively recruiting Black runaways and enslaved people to bolster their own military strength. Britain had no qualms starting a slave insurrection—or at least the threat of one—to win the war against the United States.

The British threat via Spanish lands was not just in Jackson's head. Just two months after the Creek annihilation at Horseshoe Bend, a massive British cargo of weapons, powder, food, and supplies landed in West Florida. It was all earmarked for the Creek War. Had these supplies arrived earlier (or if the Creeks had delayed their war), the entire southern Gulf theater would have been radically altered. (A major cause of American success in the Red Stick War was superior arms. Who knows what would have happened if the Red Creeks been similarly armed. How would the United States have fared against British troops plus several thousand well-armed Creeks, plus a sizeable contingent of British-trained and armed Black troops?)[123]

Regardless of their tardy appearance, the weapons and supplies were distributed to Creek warriors who were eager to continue the fight. The shipment included a number of carbines. British Captain Hugh Pigot had requested the smaller guns so Natives aged ten to fourteen could also participate in the war on Americans.[124] There was no doubt in Jackson's mind that the Native aide was the prelude to a much larger British invasion.

Jackson was right.

On August 14, 1814, the British landed in Pensacola and assumed de facto control of the town. Although only one hundred British soldiers had landed, the commanding officer, Major Edward Nicolls, quickly recruited five hundred Natives and one hundred Black men to supplement his forces. The British now had a base from which to supply the Natives more effectively and a beachhead on which they could land a much larger force that would retake Mobile and capture New Orleans.

Jackson was incensed. He demanded that Governor Manrique expel both the British and hostile Natives. When the governor refused, Jackson planned to do the task himself—and take Pensacola in the process.

Jackson marched south at the head of 4,100 men, regulars, militia, and 750 Choctaw and Chickasaw allies. On November 6, he sent an officer under a flag of truce to Manrique. The officer was fired on and beat a hasty retreat. A second emissary arrived before Manrique with Jackson's demand: the British must leave; American forces would take control of Pensacola's forts. Manrique refused, and both sides prepared for battle.

Over the next week, Manrique asked the British for help defending Pensacola, and then he rejected any foreign aid. Then he asked again that Britain provide all possible assistance in resisting the Americans, only to then refuse help and warn Britain about compromising Spain's neutrality. Just before Jackson attacked the town, Manrique made one last attempt to succor British military aid. Although Nicolls remained behind to help, the British admiral had had enough of the Spanish governor's vacillating. The best he would do now was fire on Jackson's forces from the safety of the bay.

Meanwhile, Jackson's men camped on the west side of the city, exactly where the Spanish (and British ships) expected them to attack. Nearly all the Spanish fortifications and cannons consequently faced west. In the middle of the night, Jackson snuck all but five hundred of his men through the forest and aligned them on Pensacola's eastern front just before the sun rose.

Both the Spanish and British were startled when Jackson's men attacked the town from the east. His columns were so close to the town that the British fleet was able to fire only a few rushed rounds before the Americans were in the town. Not wanting to damage Pensacola itself, the British ceased firing. The few British troops under Nicolls in town promptly withdrew. The surprised Spanish managed to place two cannons in the street, but these were quickly taken by Jackson's lead units. Within minutes, the battle was over. Governor Manrique surrendered both the town and the forts to Jackson.

Forts Barrancas and Santa Rosa, however, did not cooperate. Jackson prepared to take the harbor forts the following morning. During the interval, Britain evacuated its remaining forces and blew up both forts before sailing away, leaving Pensacola's harbor defenseless.

At the cost of five dead and ten wounded, Jackson denied the British use of the Gulf's most extensive shelter. In the process, he also scattered the hostile Native tribes who had begun to flock to Pensacola with the expectation of rendezvousing with the British army.

In short, Jackson's illegal invasion of neutral territory and subsequent victory over British and Spanish forces turned the tide of the Gulf campaign. British Admiral Alexander Cochrane would later write to General John

Lambert, "The attack made by the Americans on Pensacola has in a great measure retarded this service [the British Gulf offensive.]"[125]

Jackson soon learned that, denied both Mobile and Pensacola, Admiral Cochrane now planned a direct assault on New Orleans.

Soon after capturing Pensacola, Jackson was once again on the move, this time leading a small but victorious army to the Crescent City.

29

ACROSS OCEAN, SEA, AND GULF

George Robert Gleig
September 15–November 26, 1814

After the destruction of Washington, D.C., and the failure at Baltimore, including the campaign-altering death of General Ross, the British moved their Mid-Atlantic army toward Jamaica in preparation for the third phase of their grand 1814 plan: the sack of New Orleans.

The fleet traveled to the Caribbean as a convoy on account of American privateers, who, with Baltimore still an extant base, would no doubt be roaming the seas.[126] The journey got off to a quick and auspicious start. Gleig recorded:

> *The wind was fair, and we made great progress, insomuch that before dark the high land of St. Domingo on one side and the mountains of Cuba on the other, were discernible. In spite of the heat, therefore, our voyage soon became truly delightful. Secure of getting on under the influence of the trade winds, we had nothing to distract our thoughts, or keep us from feasting our eyes upon the glorious shores of these two islands.*[127]

Along the way, Gleig and his comrades were entertained when someone spotted a shark. Quickly, a large hook baited with salt pork was tossed overboard. The shark took the bait and then dove deep into the water as the impromptu fishermen gave it plenty of slack. Meanwhile, a boat was lowered, and when the exhausted shark finally broke the surface, it was lassoed and raised on deck.

Gleig and the other curious landlubbers gathered around as the shark put up a vicious fight. Finally, an experienced sailor chopped off the shark's tail and calmed it instantly—that is until it was gutted and disemboweled, at which point, the doomed animal resumed its struggle, repeatedly snapping at a nearby tool bag.

When the bloody scene finally culminated, the tail was cooked and served to Gleig and the other officers.[128]

Not long after Gleig's ship defeated the shark, a far more dangerous foe appeared on the horizon: an American privateer. At this point in the voyage, Gleig was part of only a two-boat convoy. What followed next was a bloody cat and mouse game of survival. After exchanging numerous rounds and successfully resisting an American boarding party, the British drove the privateer off, briefly gave pursuit, and then rerouted to its initial destination: Jamaica.

Cuba and Saint-Domingue receded in the background, and Gleig's ship arrived at Jamaica. The excited lieutenant recorded:

> [S]*eldom has landscape appeared more attractive to the eyes of a voyager, than the romantic shores of Jamaica now appeared to ours....* [E]*arly in the morning, while yet the mists hung upon their summits and concealed* [the hills], *no prospect can be imagined more sublime than that which they presented. It was, in truth, a glorious scene; and as the wind blew light and uncertain, we were permitted, from the slowness of the ship's progress, to enjoy it to the full.*[129]

The beauty of Jamaica was countered by its heat. Gleig would later write: "Of the intense heat in this place, none but those who have experienced it can form a notion. It is impossible to walk out with any comfort, except before the sun has risen, or after he has set."[130]

Nevertheless, Gleig enjoyed his brief sojourn on the island. For the first few days, there were plenty of balls and entertainments to attend. But the ever adventurous and curious Gleig wanted to see more of the island with the beautiful mountains. He hired a guide to take him to the Blue Mountains, thirty miles northeast of Kingston. It was a trip Gleig would remember fondly decades later, most particularly the fireflies, of which he wrote, "[Fireflies fill the air] like sparks from a smith's anvil when he is beating a bar of red-hot iron....Not two, or three, but thousands of these creatures dance around, filling the air with a wavering and uncertain glimmer, of the extreme beauty of which no words can convey an adequate conception."[131]

A birds'-eye view of New Orleans, created around 1858. *Beinecke Library at Yale University.*

Gleig returned to Port Royal filled with an awe and appreciation for all the beauty he had seen. But almost immediately, his thoughts were drawn to carnage and war, for Admiral Cochrane had arrived in the harbor along with a convoy of sizeable reinforcements. Soon, Gleig and all the sailors and soldiers knew that New Orleans was their destination. Two days after Cochrane's arrival, on November 26, the expeditionary force set sail.

George Robert Gleig would sail across another body of water, experience another part of the North American continent, traipse through another exotic locale, and fight yet another bloody battle. This hyperconscious warrior-observer would once again be thrust into adventure and horror, blood and beauty.

30

THE LAFFITES' BIG GAMBLE

THE BROTHERS LAFFITE
DECEMBER 1814

Two weeks after Pierre "escaped" from prison, the Laffite base in Barataria was raided by U.S. Naval Commander Daniel Todd Patterson. The entire Baratarian fleet was captured or destroyed. The Laffites were quickly running out of options.

However, just before his base was raided, Jean had hidden some valuable materiel in the swamps.

JEAN STROLLED CONFIDENTLY THROUGH the Quarter and approached Jackson's headquarters on Royal Street. He requested a meeting with the general, who was stunned by the pirate's audacity. But he was also impressed. Like the defeated Red Stick William Weatherford, who rode into Jackson's camp eight months before, this Jean Laffite had courage. Jackson had the authority to arrest him on the spot. Instead, he decided to listen.

Jean offered Jackson what he most needed: war materiel. Jackson had the men and expected more daily. Most of the men had weapons. But what he desperately needed were gun flints. He had just written to the secretary of war complaining about the lack of supplies, flints in particular, without which the guns were useless. Now, this pirate Jackson had refused to accept into his army was offering him not only 7,500 flints but also the services of his fellow Baratarians, many of whom were experienced gunners.[132]

A conference between Andrew Jackson, Jean Lafitte, and William C.C. Claiborne, from *The Pirates Own Book* (1837). *Internet Archive.*

In exchange, Laffite asked for a general amnesty for all Baratarians, most notably, his brother, Pierre.

Penned into a corner and impressed by the courage of Jean, Jackson accepted the offer. If the Baratarians upheld their end of the bargain, Jackson would do everything in his power to convince President Madison to pardon the pirate-smugglers.

Four dozen Baratarians, released from prison and materializing from the swamps, flocked to Jackson's standard.

31

REVOLUTION, REVENGE, AND RETURN TO AMERICA

PETER ELLIS BEAN
NOVEMBER 1811–DECEMBER 1814

While in his third stint in the Acapulco prison, Bean was offered release on one condition: join the King's army and help put down the popular Republican uprising that was threatening His Majesty's rule over Mexico.

A staunch Republican and enemy of Spain himself, Bean enlisted. He was given a rifle and placed on the front lines in the defense of Acapulco. Bean's release was a gross miscalculation by the Spanish government. Bean almost immediately defected. He became an indispensable aid to the rebel General José María Morelos. Bean's knowledge of gunpowder and munitions proved invaluable, and he quickly rose to the rank of colonel in the Republican army. Bean's career in Mexico paralleled that of the famous Morelos, and he was involved in nearly every battle the general was: Tenancingo, Zitlala, Huahuapen, Orizaba, Oaxaca, and Acapulco. Along the way, he avenged himself on two guards who had been especially cruel to him in the Acapulco prison, but in the process, he suffered a serious spear wound in his thigh, one that filled his boot with blood. Yet Bean got back in the saddle and led his troops. Within a week, he had captured the governor of Acapulco—the man who had sentenced him to all those cruel years in prison—and sent him, wounded, into the same prison to die.[133]

Bean became such a trusted aid to Morelos, that the general sent him on a mission to the United States to solicit funds for the cash-strapped revolutionaries and promote an American invasion of Mexican Texas.

Acapulco, as depicted in the early 1600s. *Rijksmuseum.*

Bean acquiesced and traveled to the East Coast, where he planned to sail to New Orleans. While preparing his schooner to sail, he saw one of the Laffites' schooners, *Tiger*, flying the colors of Cartagena, captained by Dominique You, out in the bay. Bean then watched the approach of a British brig, which had been offered $2,000 by Spain to capture the *Tiger*. Schooner and brig exchanged shots until the latter was disabled and Captain You sailed to safety.

Two days later, a peasant woman, while selling eggs and birds to Bean and his crew, informed them that a schooner was in the shallows six miles north. Believing it to be a Spanish ship intent on landing forces to waylay him, Bean moved north and set an ambush for the schooner. To his surprise, the floundering schooner belonged not to Spain but to Dominique You. After their victory/escape from the British brig, You's crew celebrated with the liquor aboard and ran the *Tiger* aground.

Bean sailed his own schooner out to offer help and exchange information. For the first time, he learned that the United States was at war with Great Britain. A handful of You's men joined Bean as he sailed to New Orleans.[134]

Bean landed on Cat Island, met with Jean Laffite, and gathered more detailed and up-to-date information regarding the ongoing war. Bean left

The New Orleans docks, by John Bachmann (1857). *Library of Congress.*

the schooner in Laffite's care and made his way into New Orleans, where he met with his old Tennessee acquaintance, Governor Claiborne. Bean then journeyed to Natchez, where he hoped to gather money, war materiel, and soldiers for his revolution. His timing could not have been worse. The current war, in particular, the present Gulf invasion, had drained America's reserves, both fiscal and human. Simply put, there was neither money nor soldiers to spare for a separate foreign conflict, especially one that would pit the United States against Spain, a nation that controlled Pensacola and still held influence over the Gulf's Native tribes. The United States desperately needed Spain to remain neutral until Great Britain was neutralized.

Bean returned to New Orleans. The next day, he learned that the American gunboats guarding the eastern approaches to the city had been captured by the British. There was no doubt New Orleans was the next target.

32

LAKE BORGNE

Daniel Todd Patterson
December 8–14, 1814

Commodore Patterson received word from his only lieutenant at sea, Thomas ap Catesby Jones, that the forty-gun British frigate *Armide* had been sighted in the Gulf. New Orleans, after all, was the British objective.

With a squadron too small to resist the British fleet, Jones opted to serve as the maritime eyes of Patterson and Jackson and delay the British as long as possible. As long as his boats were in the area, the British could not disembark. So, Jones withdrew his squadron of a sloop, a schooner, and five gunboats to Bay St. Louis, roughly sixty miles east of New Orleans. Jones had a combined force of 204 men and 25 guns.[135]

Patterson had taken an enormous gamble by sending the bulk of his ships into the waters between New Orleans and Mobile. As a consequence, he had only two ships with which to defend the Crescent City: the *Louisiana* and *Carolina*. But so much value did he—and Jackson—place on intelligence, that he perceived the gamble worth the potential consequences.

Meanwhile, Jones was left to face a fleet of 45 boats, 42 cannons, and 1,200 soldiers.

December 13, 1814

The British flotilla, under Captain Nicholas Lockyer, made its way to Pass Christian and continued to sail toward Bay St. Louis. Jones now knew for sure that they were determined to destroy his squadron before disembarking. Against such formidable odds, Jones again withdrew, this time west toward Malheureux Island.

As they made their escape, Jones's crew saw a terrific explosion over Bay St. Louis. One of Jones's seven boats, the schooner *Seahorse*, with its one cannon and fourteen men, had been removing valuable materiel and gotten trapped in the process. Rather than let his schooner fall into enemy hands, the captain torched both boat and warehouse. Jones was now down one boat.

Then the wind slackened. A little after midnight, it died entirely.

DECEMBER 14, 1814

Jones was left with two options: torch his fleet and lead his men to join his commander in New Orleans or stay and fight. The odds were bleak: 190 men in 6 gunboats against 45 boats carrying 1,200 soldiers.

Jones decided to fight. He sent word to Patterson and prepared to trade blood for time.

The *Alligator*, the ship that delivered word of Jones's plight to Patterson and carried a four-pound cannon and eight men, had run ashore, leaving Jones with one less boat. He ordered his five remaining boats to form a line between Malheureux Island and the mainland, their larger guns pointing toward the British boats.

Captain Lockyer quickly captured the *Alligator* and then sailed directly at Jones, whose ship held the middle of the American line.

The battle was bloody and brutal. The British boats took a beating from the larger American guns, but there were simply too many British boats still afloat. They swarmed around Jones.

The fate of Lockyer's boat was indicative of the hand-to-hand fighting that would determine the day. Lockyer received three wounds, and most of his officers were killed. The boat next to him sank entirely. More successful was the boat led by Lieutenant George Pratt, the officer who had placed the first burning torch to the U.S. Capitol four months prior. Pratt managed to board Jones's boat, only to be promptly shot—and shot again, and again, and again, and again. Still, he stumbled, sword and pistol in hand, across the American flagship. Jones himself fired point-blank at Pratt. But the Brit refused to die. By the battle's end, he had suffered twelve bullet wounds. He

Combat Naval dans la Baie d'Algésiras, 5 Juillet 1801, by Antoine Roux (1838). *Library of Congress.*

continued to battle death another three weeks before he finally succumbed to the inevitable. One boarder had his leg blown off, another lost both his legs, one was shot through the eye, and yet another was killed when a pike punctured his lungs. Others were struck by cannonballs that American sailors had hoisted with them as they climbed the rigging and then thrown down on the British beneath.[136]

Despite the horrific slaughter, the British pressed on. Lockyer eventually boarded the now-wounded Jones's flagship and turned the guns on the American boat next to him. Within five minutes, the other four ships struck their colors.

Seventy-seven British sailors had been killed or wounded along with forty-one Americans. Every living American was taken prisoner and sent to the prison ship the *Plantagenet*.[137]

British losses had been high, but of the nine American gunboats near New Orleans, one was now sunk and six were in possession of the British navy. More importantly, a landing could now be executed unmolested.

With only a schooner and a sloop left—the *Carolina* and *Louisiana*—Patterson would need to combine practical wisdom with aggressive daring if he hoped to avenge the loss of the flotilla he had entrusted to Jones.

PART II

THE FINAL ACT

33

ON THE EVE OF BATTLE

DECEMBER 22, 1814

Commodore Patterson, still smarting from the loss of Jones's flotilla but with two armed boats still afloat, hoped that the two American forts along the Mississippi River would keep Admiral Cochrane's powerful fleet at bay so he could play some role in the defense of New Orleans.

Peter Ellis Bean, recently escaped from years of captivity in Mexican prisons and now a member of Jackson's staff, waited alongside the general, eager to contribute to the defense of New Orleans in the hopes that the United States would reciprocate by contributing to the freeing of Mexico from regal Spanish rule.[138]

Reuben Kemper, distraught over his brother Samuel's recent passing in camp, sat with his comrades from Mississippi, spoiling for a fight against yet another imperial foe that threatened his lands.

Pierre Laffite worked with Commodore Patterson at Fort St. John, erecting batteries to protect the Bayou St. John approach to New Orleans. His brother, Jean, carried a message from Jackson to Major Reynolds at the Bayou St. Denis defense that ordered him to send fifty men to the Laffites' old Baratarian base to further obstruct any British approach from that direction.[139]

Arsène Lacarrière-Latour, who had helped General Wilkinson, years before, map the seven potential approaches an enemy army might use in an assault on New Orleans, waited at Jackson's side to see which approach(es) the British would utilize.[140]

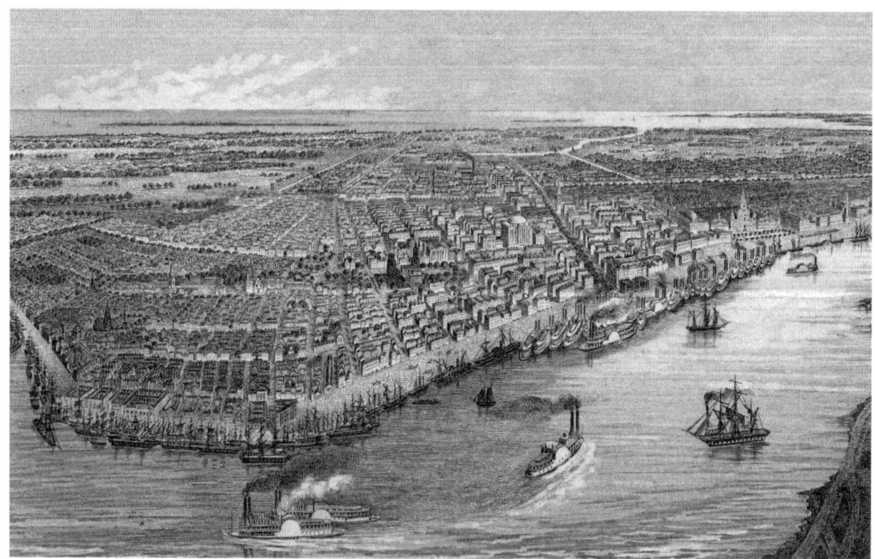

An 1857 illustration of New Orleans, by Louis Schwarz. *Beinecke Library at Yale University.*

And General Andrew Jackson, weakened by dysentery and his previous wounds, spent another nerve-wracking day waiting for reliable information on which he could act. No doubt, New Orleans was the British objective, and Jackson believed he had obstructed all possible routes. He expected to have plenty of advance warning to move his army into the most favorable of positions to greet the empire that had taken so much from him nearly four decades prior.

34

THE LANDING

DECEMBER 22–23, 1814
11:00 A.M.–4:00 A.M.

It was a frosty morning, two days before Christmas, and the Villere plantation was sleepily coming to life. Oak and pecan trees surrounded the wide gallery that, in turn, surrounded the spacious one-story house. An avenue of trees led to the levee half a mile away, and a garden and groves of lemon and orange trees filled the air with their fragrant scents.

Major Gabriel Villere sat on his porch, smoking a morning cigar. He had been ordered by General Jackson to obstruct the Bienvenue Canal, which ran to his father's plantation, and to keep a vigilant eye out for any possible British approach. Villere had become one of Jackson's many invaluable eyes. But the Villeres had business with the Laffites, and the canal he was asked to obstruct was often used by the brothers to bring their smuggled goods to men like Gabriel Villere. In the end, Bayou Bienvenue was left open.

Gabriel had at least sent a detachment of seven men to the bayou's entrance. The sentries brought a deck of cards with them, and the bayou remained unwatched—unwatched and unobstructed.

Meanwhile, Lieutenant George Robert Gleig and the 85th Infantry, along with the 95th, embarked on open boats on Pea Island and began their twenty-five-mile journey across open water to the head of Bayou Bienvenue. Because of the loss of Patterson's gunboats on Lake Borgne, the crossing would be unimpeded. Yet the British command had entirely misjudged the weather. Remembering the fate of the French soldiers in the tropical Saint-Domingue summer and determined to avoid the hurricane season, Admiral Cochrane decided to attack New Orleans in December, when he expected temperate weather. Instead, it was unusually bitterly cold. Now, the first wave of his troops, led by a Creole fisherman and two of Nicolls's Choctaws, rowed across open water, a light but freezing drizzle making the crossing torturous. The other units waited their turn on Pea Island. Even with Patterson's captured boats in tow, there were not enough transports and shallow-draft boats to transport the army at once. So, the remaining units waited their turn. (It was especially torturous for the five-hundred-man 5th West Indian Regiment, a Black unit of Caribbean soldiers whom Cochrane had brought along to garrison New Orleans once the city was captured, thereby keeping his white troops safe from the summer diseases that had killed so many in the Caribbean.)[141]

Despite the discomfort and danger of the weather, the crossing went relatively smoothly. The British had dispatched an advance party to capture or kill the American sentries Villere had sent to the head of the bayou. The party split into two groups, one silently rowing above the shack holding the card-playing Americans and one below. Lieutenant Gleig described the capture of the critical outpost:

> [N]*o persons could be less on their guard than the party here stationed. The officer who conducted the force sent against them, found not so much as a single sentinel posted; but having landed his men at two places, above and below the hut which they inhabited, extended his ranks so as to surround it, and closing gradually in, took them all fast asleep, without noise or resistance.*[142]

With the sentry silenced, the British advance guard began sailing up the bayou. The water level, however, was lower than expected. The first barge was rowed and punted as far as it could go but was eventually grounded. All the remaining barges, in single file, came to an abrupt halt. The soldiers, not wanting to wade through frigid swamp water, formed a long bridge and slowly walked single file from boat to boat until they stood on relatively dry land.

Now, the march began. The soldiers had sat for hours as they were rowed across Lake Borgne and up Bayou Bienvenue, and then they waited, freezing, in the barges, hemmed in by cane, as the Royal Engineers cleared a path toward dry land. And then they waited even longer as one boatload of soldiers after another made their way across the narrow impromptu bridge. But the men now faced another task: silently trekking across soggy land, surrounded by seven-foot-tall cane.

Lieutenant Gleig later recalled the scene:

> *The place where we landed was as wild as possible to imagine. Wherever we looked, nothing was to be seen except one huge marsh, covered with tall reeds; not a house, not a vestige of human industry could be discovered; and even of trees, there were but a few growing upon the banks of the creek. Yet it was such a spot as above all others, favoured our operations. No eye could watch us, or report our arrival to the American General. By remaining quietly among the reeds, we might effectually conceal ourselves from notice; because, from the appearance of all around, it was easy to perceive the place which we occupied was seldom, if ever before marked with a human footstep.*[143]

The empty boats now rowed backward, one by one, until they again reached Lake Borgne, where they began the twenty-five-mile journey back to Pea Island to pick up another batch of soldiers. This process continued all night and into the next day.

Laborious step by laborious step, the soldiers of the 85th and 95th advanced. Finally, the lead units emerged from the swamp and stood beneath a grove of cypress trees. Half a mile away stood the levee and the road to New Orleans. In between lay the Villere plantation.[144]

Colonel William Thornton and his men advanced at the double-quick into position and surrounded the Villere home. Gabriel noticed the red-coated soldiers hurrying toward his house. He immediately ran to the back door, where he was met by a detachment of British soldiers and was arrested along with his brother and twenty-six others.[145]

Villere was in a doubly precarious position—a prisoner and a potential traitor. His house had been surrounded, and he was now under guard because he had disobeyed Jackson's explicit orders to obstruct the bayou. A British army was now nine miles from New Orleans, undetected, because of him.[146]

Hoping to rectify the situation, he waited until his guards were distracted and then jumped out an open window onto the gallery and then to the ground. Musket balls flew by him as he ran toward the cypress swamp. But Villere had a head start and no musket to lug along. He quickly outran his guards and found a moss-draped tree to climb, only to realize his favorite dog had followed him. Villere promptly killed the dog with a branch, covered his body with leaves, and climbed the tree.[147]

When the coast was clear, Villere descended and made his way to the neighboring plantation, which was owned by Denis de La Ronde. The two

Cypress swamp on the Opelousas railroad, Louisiana. *Wikimedia Commons.*

quickly made their way to Jackson's headquarters and informed the general that the British had arrived. Jackson had already heard the rumors. The night before, La Ronde had reported seeing British sails in Lake Borgne. Jackson sent out scouts in search of a British landing party. He now sent Arsène Lacarrière-Latour and Major Tatum Howell to confirm the landing and gather the necessary data. They soon confirmed Villere's report. Tatum rode back to inform Jackson while Latour rode on to ascertain the situation. At 1:30 p.m., he came upon the British at Lacoste's plantation and determined their number to be 1,800.[148] Latour quickly rode back to apprise his general of the situation.

The Battle of New Orleans was now underway.

35

THE NIGHT BATTLE

DECEMBER 23–24, 1814
6:30 P.M.–4:00 A.M.

On receiving confirmation that the British had, in fact, landed a large part of their army, undetected and eight miles from New Orleans, Andrew Jackson roared, "By the Eternal! The British shall not sleep upon our territory!" And he immediately sprang into action. He summoned the troops at his nearby disposal to the Place d'Armes; 1,004 soldiers showed up, prepared to drive the British back into the Gulf.[149]

As the units were rendezvousing, Jackson, still suffering from his dueling wounds, severe dysentery, and now insomnia, ate four tablespoons of boiled rice and half a cup of coffee. He took a thirty-minute nap and then rose, determined to settle the fate of New Orleans in a winner-take-all night battle.[150] Historian William C. Davis claims, "From distant antiquity to the latest generation, a timeless measure of leadership has been a commander's response to the unexpected. Those who see opportunity through the gloom often achieve greatness."[151] Jackson would either enter the pantheon of America's greatest generals or lose his country's most important port in one deluded attack.

Jackson's battle plan was bold, impetuous, complicated, and risky. If it was successful, the beached British units would be annihilated. If it was unsuccessful, the Americans would be forced to retreat to the city, broken and demoralized. Later comments by Jackson suggest that he was prepared to burn New Orleans and its years' worth of cotton bales and other trade goods that had been accumulating in the waterfront warehouses due to the

British blockade. In short, the upcoming night battle would end in either the salvation or the death of New Orleans.

Characteristically bold, Jackson's plan consisted of a four-pronged assault. Because of Arsène Lacarrière-Latour's scouting, Jackson had a relatively good idea of the British deployment. He knew they had set a picket line between the La Ronde and Lacoste plantations, and he knew they had already landed roughly two thousand soldiers, with reinforcements continuing to be rowed across Lake Borgne. With the British sedentary and awaiting reinforcements, Jackson finalized his night assault.[152]

Commodore Patterson would send his two vessels, the *Carolina* and *Louisiana*, downriver until they were parallel with the main camp. Simultaneously, General Coffee, led by Pierre Laffite, would lead Jackson's left flank with 900 men around the swamps in a flanking/pincer movement that would push the British toward the river and the ships' cannons. Meanwhile, Jackson would lead the right flank (technically the center, with the *Carolina* operating to his right) and push straight down the middle to drive the confused and concentrated British back toward the Gulf. Finally, General David Morgan, on the west bank of the Mississippi River, guarding English Turn with 350 men, would cross the river and strike the enemy's rear, adding to the panic of the retreating British.

All four attacks were to be coordinated and executed on a cloudy and foggy night.

Meanwhile…

The British advanced to the Lacoste plantation. General John Keane established a picket line on the border of La Ronde's plantation, but having found no Americans, the soldiers were allowed to relax. Some pulled out their rations and prepared the noonday meal. Others raided the neighboring houses for food. Still others took advantage of the warming weather and went for a cleansing swim.[153]

Later that afternoon, a handful of Jackson's dragoons exchanged fire with the British pickets. At first, the sporadic fire alarmed the relaxing British soldiers, but as it died off as quickly as it had begun, the Redcoats assumed the Americans had been driven off. No need to be alarmed. The American pickets would no doubt report the British landing, but what did that matter? The last boatloads of reinforcements would be dropped off that night, and the full British army would march on New Orleans in the morning. Beauty and booty awaited.

With nothing but the brief exchange of sentry fire to disturb them, Gleig and his companions passed a pleasurable afternoon. As dusk approached, they began to prepare their evening meal. Fires crackled and the smell of roasted chickens and geese began to fill the air. Gleig even sat back and relaxed with a glass of good claret.[154]

The soldiers expected an even finer meal the following afternoon in New Orleans.

Around 7:00 p.m., Jackson's men began their descent on the unsuspecting British. The commander watched as the *Carolina*'s mast drifted silently downriver. His land units began their own march toward the enemy.

Arsène Lacarrière-Latour and Ellis Bean remained at their commander's side.

Reuben Kemper advanced with Major Thomas Hinds's dragoons and the Feliciana troop. His brother, Samuel, had died of disease while in camp seven weeks before. Reuben was eager to take out his wrath on the invading Redcoats.

Pierre Laffite, who knew well the swamps and bayous leading into New Orleans, led Coffee's unit along the swamp and around the British right flank.[155]

By 7:30 p.m., Patterson's *Carolina*, captained by John D. Henley and crewed by ninety men, most of them Laffite's Baratarians, was in place, parallel with the well-lit British camp.[156] The schooner was only three hundred yards away and armed with five six-pound cannons and two twelve-pound swivel guns.[157]

Despite the proximity of the deadly schooner, the British were not alarmed. Many assumed it was a British ship sent by Cochrane or perhaps a friendly French merchant looking to sell some food or wares to the soldiers. Lieutenant Gleig, enjoying his meal and claret, heard the anchor drop and splash.[158] Curious soldiers wandered over to the river and hailed the boat.

Silence.

And then came a thunderous roar as the *Carolina*'s seven guns belched forth deadly lead at the unsuspecting camp. The first rounds of grape tore through the soldiers gathered around their fires. Kettles were upset, stacked muskets knocked over, and limbs severed. Not too far from Gleig, a lieutenant was decapitated by chain shot. Panicked, the soldiers immediately scattered, some toward the back of the nearby houses, others, including Gleig, toward the levee, where they would be safe from the deadly projectiles.[159]

Commodore Patterson, soon after, explained the scene in a letter to the secretary of the navy:

> [A] *few minutes after, having been frequently hailed by the enemy's sentinels, anchored, veered out a long scope of cable, sheered close in shore abreast of their camp, and commenced a heavy (and as I have since learned most destructive) fire from our starboard battery, and small arms, which was returned most spiritedly by the enemy with congreve rockets and musketry from their whole force, when after about forty minutes of most incessant fire, the enemy was silenced; the fire from our battery was continued until nine o'clock upon the enemy's flank while engaged in the field with our army, at which hour ceased firing, supposing from the distance of the enemy's fire (for it was too dark to see anything on shore) that they had retreated beyond the range of our guns.*[160]

After several volleys had been fired, the British finally began to return fire, but they had no heavy guns, only three-pounders and what proved to be highly ineffective Congreve rockets. And muskets did little damage to the side of a schooner.[161] The British fire proved ineffective, and the *Carolina* remained free to fire at will. It did so until the crew heard the firing of American rifles driving the British toward the river. The *Carolina* was then ordered to cease fire for fear of hitting its own troops.[162]

As soon as Jackson and Pierre Laffite heard the opening salvo from the *Carolina*, the two wings began their march on the British pickets—Pierre leading Coffee around the flank and Jackson, with his two cannons down the center, moving along the levee road. (Presumably, Morgan was headed northeast from English Turn.)

At the same time, the boats carrying the remaining British across Lake Borgne heard *Carolina*'s broadsides twenty miles away. The sailors began to row as fast as they could to rush the reinforcements to the battle.[163]

An ambitious amphibious landing and an equally daring four-pronged assault with three independent commands were on a collision course.

The first British units to bear the brunt of Jackson's daring were the pickets at the border of Lacoste's and La Ronde's plantations. They were promptly sent running back to camp. With Patterson's schooner creating chaos and Jackson's units with the element of surprise, it looked as if the Battle of New Orleans would be a one-day affair. But a quick-thinking Colonel William Thornton ordered units from the 85th and 95th Regiments to support the pickets. British resistance stiffened.

Simultaneously, Pierre Laffite was stealthily leading the left flank along the swamp. He, too, achieved complete surprise, and the British right began to crumble and fall back toward the river.

With the continuous and increasingly nearer-to-the-river crackle of muskets and rifles, the *Carolina* ceased firing, lest it be the cause of friendly fire. The battle now evolved into two separate fronts; the collapse of either would result in a catastrophic defeat for the British.

The American Left/British Right

Pierre Laffite led Coffee's brigade right atop Gleig's unsuspecting unit. The surprised 85th promptly withdrew. But being disciplined British troops and the vanquishers of Napoleon, the unit regrouped and charged the American line. They were forced back but again regrouped in one of the Lacoste plantation's orange groves.

On the brink of being annihilated, four companies of the 21st Foot arrived just in time. Gleig later admitted, "There cannot be a doubt that we should have fallen to a man had not the arrival of fresh troops at this critical juncture turned the tide of affairs."[164]

Just as fortunate for Gleig and his comrades, Coffee and Beale's units became separated by the night and smoke. Some Brits began firing from the plantation's slave cabins, causing Coffee and his Tennesseans to charge them, and the melee became musket and bayonet against long rifle and tomahawk and knife.[165] Pierre Laffite was in the middle of it all, and Coffee would later testify to the smuggler's courage under fire.

The initial American advantage of surprise was counteracted by the British advantage of having the moon at their backs, allowing them better visibility.[166] But then the battle leveled out once the British understood the Americans were on them and fog (along with gun smoke) drifted over the battlefield. Now, neither side was advantaged. The battle devolved into pure chaos.

Making matters worse, both sides spoke the same language. Deception was rampant. John Henry Cooke of the 43rd Light Infantry recalled:

> *Such confusion took place as seldom occurs in war—the bayonet of the British and the knife of the American were in active opposition at close quarters during this eventful night.... The darkness was partially dispelled*

> *for a few moments, now and then, by flashes of fire-arms; and whenever the outlines of men were distinguishable, the Americans called out, "Don't fire, we are your friends!" prisoners were taken and retaken.*
>
> *The British soldiers likewise, hearing their mother tongue spoken, were captured by this deception; when such mistakes being detected, the nearest American received a knock-down blow; and in this manner prisoners on both sides having escaped, again joined in the fray, calling out lustily for their friends.*[167]

Lieutenant Gleig, too, experienced confusion and disorientation. His 85th Regiment was ordered to stop Coffee on the British right. As he approached the fray, Gleig noticed a detachment of soldiers in his fog-enshrouded front. Realizing the unit could belong to either side, Gleig crept forward to investigate. Believing Gleig to be another lost American, a voice called to him that they were friendly forces, lost and in search of their comrades. Gleig told them he knew exactly who they were and to stay put, that his men would escort them to their unit. He promptly returned with a small guard from the 85th and announced that the hapless Americans were now his prisoners, taking an officer's sword in the process.

Gleig prepared to march his captives toward his own lines. But at that moment, the fog lifted temporarily, and the Americans realized they had a numerical advantage. They began to pick up their guns and fight back, and another melee ensued.

Having already taken one officer's sword, Gleig demanded another's. When the American refused and turned to flee, Gleig delivered a glancing blow on the back of his head. Immediately after, another U.S. soldier thrust his bayonet at Gleig's head but pierced his collar instead. Gleig struck the soldier in the head with his sword, forcing him to flee. Having helped halt the American advance as ordered, the fortunate lieutenant led his men to the safety of his own lines.[168]

Not all British soldiers were so lucky. In the confusion, Reuben Kemper and a handful of Hind's dragoons were cut off on the far left. Using years of instincts acquired during his ongoing guerrilla war with the Spanish, Kemper sensed the enemy nearby. Musket flashes revealed three Redcoats running by. Kemper shouted above the noise of battle: "G-d D—m your souls! What do you do there?" When one replied they were looking for their regiment, Kemper inquired which regiment. On receiving their reply, he raised his rifle, shouting, "There it is, G-d D— you!" And he led the unfortunate trio toward the American line, now prisoners of war.[169]

The Center

While the Americans and British fought to turn and defend the flank, the center of the battlefield was up for grabs.

Just as he had on his right and left flanks, Jackson had achieved near total surprise in the center. His wing had sent the British sentries flying, and his cannons joined the *Carolina* in spreading death and chaos among the unsuspecting enemy camp.

However, a quick-thinking Colonel William Thornton immediately grasped the severity of the situation and sent Marines to reinforce the British center. So prompt and disciplined were the Redcoats that Jackson's wing quickly found itself in a dogfight.

The British Marines charged Jackson's only two land cannons and were on the verge of capturing them when Jackson rode to the front amid bullets, shouting, "Save the guns, my boys, at every sacrifice!"[170] Whether foolish or brave, Jackson's action saved the cannons and the American center, as his 7th Regiment rushed forward and stymied the British counterattack.

The cannons were saved but were now essentially useless; the battle in the center had also devolved into pockets of men fighting in the foggy dark, hoping it was the enemy they were firing at.

Although he was hoping to deliver a decisive blow to the British and drive them back into the Gulf, Jackson realized he had done enough that night. To attempt more would be to place his entire army in jeopardy. At 9:30 p.m., he ordered his men to withdraw to their original position on the Lacoste plantation. The British advance had been stopped, and he had placed his army between the enemy and New Orleans, but British reinforcements were still being landed.

The last fighting that night occurred when General David Morgan marched his 350 men from English Turn to the Jumonville plantation at 11:30 p.m. His men fired some ineffectual shots at the British outposts and withdrew to English Turn at dawn.[171]

At 4:00 a.m., with his troops reassembled at the Lacoste plantation, Jackson finally withdrew from the field of battle. He led his men two miles west to the Rodriguez Canal. He would now shift his strategy from the offensive to the defensive.

The night attack of December 23 lasted less than two hours. It was fought over one square mile of plantations and ditches.[172] The official British report listed 46 killed, 167 wounded, and 64 missing. On the American side, Arsène Lacarrière-Latour reported 24 killed, 115 wounded, and 74 imprisoned.[173]

Battle of New Orleans, by N. Currier (1842). *Library of Congress.*

Latour would later add his own reflection on the importance of his commander's night attack:

> *The result of the affair of the 23^d was the saving of Louisiana; for it cannot be doubted but that the enemy, had he not been attacked with such impetuosity, when he had hardly effected his disembarkation, would, at that very night, or early next morning, have marched against the city, which was not then covered by any fortification, and was defended by hardly five thousand men, mostly militia, who could not, in the open field, have withstood disciplined troops, accustomed to the use of the bayonet, a weapon with which most of the militia were unprovided.*[174]

Whether Jackson had saved New Orleans with his daring actions on the night of December 23 or the British had successively repulsed a surprise attack, held their ground, and driven the enemy from the field was now a moot point. The element of surprise, held by both armies at one point in the preceding twenty-four hours, was now lost to both. Each commander now grasped the situation. The British objective lay six miles to the west. In between stood Jackson's army, now digging into a field three-quarters of a mile wide. An impenetrable swamp lay to the right of the British, and the Mississippi River lay to their left. With Jackson ahead and the Gulf behind, there was only one way to New Orleans: through the Chalmette plantation.

36

RECONNAISSANCE IN FORCE

DECEMBER 28, 1814

With both sides claiming victory the night of December 23, the next four days passed relatively uneventfully—except for those on the picket line, who lived under the constant anxiety of imminent death. General Edward Pakenham arrived on December 25, buoying the morale of his rain-soaked and cold troops. Surely the hero of Salamanca would have his men bivouacked in comfortable, exotic New Orleans within a day or two.

Pakenham, however, was not pleased with the upper command, stating, "I regret the defeat of our forces due to the error made on the 23rd of December. Our troops should have advanced to New Orleans immediately on taking Villere's plantation."[175] He understood that he was now bottlenecked on flat land and flanked by an impenetrable swamp and the Mississippi River. He suggested withdrawing and landing the army in a more favorable location, but Admiral Cochrane and his staff convinced Pakenham to stay. After all, it was predominantly militia between him and his objective. The Americans would flee, just as they had at Bladensburg.[176] Pakenham relented and agreed to take the American position via a frontal assault.

But first, he would have to eliminate the *Louisiana* and *Carolina*, which had been harassing the British line since the night assault, killing some and psychologically torturing the rest. Furthermore, if the sloop-of-war and schooner were not eliminated, they would lay down a devastating enfilade fire as Pakenham's troops marched on Jackson's line.

Pakenham ordered six cannons, two howitzers, and a mortar rowed and dragged sixty miles by boat and through swamp until they reached the levee. Under cover of night, the British gunners established their gun carriages. Fortunately for Pakenham, his commander of artillery was a fellow victor at Salamanca, Colonel Alexander Dickson. Dickson had utilized hot shot effectively at Salamanca and now proposed to do the same in Louisiana.[177] His guns were not likely to win an artillery duel with Patterson's schooners, but by erecting a furnace and heating the balls ahead of time, Dickson gained the advantage on the wooden boats.

Between 2:00 and 7:00 a.m., the furnace heated the projectiles. When day revealed the *Carolina*, Dickson opened fire.

Commodore Patterson ordered the *Carolina* to move to safety, parallel with Jackson's new line. Patterson had recently established himself aboard the *Louisiana* and began moving it to safety. However, strong winds prevented the *Carolina* from joining its sister ship.[178]

After only the second round of British fire, the *Carolina* was aflame. It immediately became clear that the powder room had been compromised, and the sailors leapt overboard and began rowing for shore. Two and a half hours later, the schooner exploded in a deafening roar.[179] Lieutenant Gleig expressed the emotions of his fellow soldiers: "In itself, the sight was a fine one, but to us it was peculiarly gratifying, for we could not but experience something like satiated revenge at the destruction of a vessel from which we had suffered so much damage."[180] No doubt, Colonel Nicolls's Native allies were impressed by the sheer size of the explosion.

The *Louisiana* was next. Fortunately for the Americans, Patterson had already begun moving the sloop up the Mississippi River. Unfortunately, there was no wind. So, the Baratarians, the "hellish banditti" Jackson had enlisted in the final hour and the men Commodore Patterson had so ruthlessly persecuted, went to work. One hundred Baratarians attached hawsers and, by brute strength, towed the schooner to safety as hot shot and balls rained down on them.[181] Half a mile later, the *Louisiana* was safely alongside Jackson's line, ready to rake the British from the side.

Dickson's assault had neutralized one gunboat and destroyed the other. However, his bombardment had been costly. He had used between a quarter and a third of his shot, ammunition that would become critical to Pakenham's success in the days to come.[182] In addition, the *Louisiana* had been hit only once and was positioned to render Jackson invaluable service in the event of a frontal assault. And while the *Carolina* was at the bottom of the Mississippi River, only one of its men had been killed and six wounded.

The rest of the crew, including a number of invaluable gunners, were saved and repositioned along Jackson's lines, eager for revenge.[183]

With his left flank now secure, Pakenham was ready to move toward New Orleans. However, he still had precious little intelligence. How many men did the Americans have? How strong was Jackson's line? Where was it weakest?

Not yet ready for a winner-take-all frontal assault, the hero of Salamanca elected to gather intelligence via a reconnaissance in force. If the reconnaissance found the vital American weakness, it could just as easily turn into a victorious march into the Crescent City.

A full-scale reconnaissance was necessary because of the activity along the British picket lines. The night after his arrival, Pakenham attempted to gather information himself along the front. He saw the Feliciana troop and Hind's dragoons, Reuben Kemper in tow, standing and trotting and galloping along the field, eyes on the enemy. A disgusted Pakenham noted the attire and unmilitary bearing "of snipe and rabbit hunters beating the bushes for game."[184]

American forces attacked the British sentries all night. In fact, they had been doing so each night since the night attack on December 23. They would continue to do so each night the British remained east of New Orleans.

Lieutenant Gleig himself was fired on by American snipers from a thicket one night as he checked on his sentries around 1:00 a.m.[185] Gleig emphatically condemned the tactics used by "uncivilized" men like Reuben Kemper and his fellow "dirty shirts."

> *Those savages have no knowledge how war should be fought. In Europe, when two armies face each other, the outposts of neither are molested. Nay, so far is the tacit good understanding carried out that I myself have seen French and English sentinels not more than twenty yards apart. These "dirty shirts" entertain no such chivalric notions.*[186]

On a much more approving note, Arsène Lacarrière-Latour wrote of the American assaults on British outposts:

> *The Tennesseans, on account of their well-known skill with the rifle, were the terror of the British sentinels and advanced posts. Their uniform, consisting of a brown hunting dress, rendered it difficult to perceive them among the underwood and dry grass through which they approached to shoot down British sentinels, whom they never missed.*[187]

General Coffee's men, too, engaged in the night escapades, in which his Choctaw warriors proved at least as adept as his Tennesseans in inflicting fear—and a few casualties—among the British sentries.

As Jackson's irregulars were harassing the British sentries by night, his men were preparing a more effective punishment by day.

So relentless were Jackson's tireless efforts to prepare his lines that his aides worried for his well-being. As Jackson was already suffering from his duels and racked by dysentery and insomnia, many feared Old Hickory was working himself into an early grave. When advised to slow his pace, Jackson snapped back, "No, sir: there's no knowing when nor where these rascals will attack. They shall not catch me unprepared. When we have driven the d—d red coat villains into the swamp, there will be time enough to sleep."[188]

With the passing of each hour, Jackson's line grew deeper, longer, and stronger. Pierre Laffite made one of the most prescient suggestions of the campaign when he advised Jackson to extend his line deeper into the swamp and bend it back about two hundred yards to ensure he would not be flanked. Jackson strengthened all approaches to his line by building a redoubt in front

British troops during the Battle of New Orleans, with the death of Major General Packenham (1817). *Library of Congress.*

of his right flank, along the levee road. The redoubt would add a second layer of protection to his right and provide enfilading fire across his line's front.[189] Jackson hoped to protect his center with a withering crossfire along with the guns from the *Louisiana*.

With his line strengthening with each thrust of the shovel, Jackson still needed reliable men to protect that line, especially artillerymen. Pierre Laffite, whom Jackson had only recently promised to pardon—and even more recently begun to respect and trust—suggested that the general summon the pirates/smugglers Renaldo Beluche and Dominique You from sentinel duty at Fort St. John to the main front. Jackson did so, and an additional twenty Baratarians were assigned to Battery no. 3 near the center of Jackson's line.[190]

Old Hickory also ordered his men to clear the line of sight in front of his earthworks and to burn the buildings on Bienvenue plantation.[191]

Should—nay, when—Pakenham advanced, Jackson wanted plenty of open space, where cannons, rifles, and muskets could do their damage before his line was reached.

DECEMBER 28

By December 28, Pakenham was ready to gather what information he could and, if a weakness could be exploited, to march on New Orleans itself. In the event of the latter, the general ordered his men to carry two days' rations to the reconnaissance.[192] Pakenham's strategy was to march one brigade down the levee road against Jackson's right and another along the swamps to Jackson's left.

American pickets had already burned the buildings and cane between them and the advancing British, giving their cannons a clear line of sight.

At seven hundred yards, the Americans behind Jackson's line got their first sight of the advancing Redcoats.[193] The American cannons roared into action. Pakenham's left flank was stymied by the relentless American artillery. Britain responded with Congreve rockets. The discrepancy between the two projectiles was obvious. American balls cut down British troops, while British rockets simply startled the Americans—at first.

Robert Remini gave an excellent description of these novel weapons hitherto unseen by the American backwoodsmen: "They rose with a great swooshing sound and seemed to dart from one side to another, and when they fell to the ground, they would slither through the cane stubble like snakes and finally explode with a sharp report and a gush of acrid smoke."[194]

Sensing his men's initial terror, Jackson rode along his line, shouting reassurances: "Pay no attention to the rockets, boys, they are mere toys to amuse children!"[195] Soon enough, the terror of the rockets was replaced with mild contempt. Latour reported, "They hoped that its very noise would strike terror into us; but we soon grew accustomed to it, and thought it little formidable; for in the whole course of the campaign, the rockets only wounded ten men, and blew up two caissons."[196]

It must have come as no surprise to Gleig and his comrades that the Congreve rockets had such little effect, for they had seen the weapons' failure at the bombardment of Fort McHenry, where Francis Scott Key was inspired by the "the rockets' red glare, the bombs bursting in air."

The American cannons, on the other hand, did considerable damage. Gleig would later write:

> *That the Americans are excellent marksmen, as well with artillery as with rifles, we have had frequent cause to acknowledge; but, perhaps, on no occasion did they assert their claim to the title of good artillerymen more effectively than on the present. Scarce a ball passed over, or fell short of its mark, but all striking full into the midst of our ranks, occasioned terrible havoc.*[197]

Despite the deadly American barrage, Pakenham's reconnaissance nearly breached the left side of Jackson's line. The American general had placed so much attention on the levee road and overestimated the protection provided by the cypress swamp that Pakenham's right under General Gibbs nearly broke the line. In fact, Gibbs might have been at the point of turning Jackson's flank when he received orders to withdraw.

Pakenham, however, had little choice, for his left was being decimated by a crossfire from the *Louisiana* and Jackson's batteries to the front. During the seven hours of the reconnaissance, the *Louisiana* fired eight hundred shells at the approaching and then stagnant British.[198] At the same time, the eight batteries from Jackson's line poured a withering and constant fire on their counterparts.[199] So concentrated was the American fire that Pakenham ordered his left flank off the levee road and into a cane field to seek what cover they could. He also ordered his own cannons forward to either silence the American guns or create a breach in the line. Within half an hour of arriving, three British cannons were disabled.[200]

Jackson during the Battle of New Orleans, by F.C. Yohn (1922). *Library of Congress.*

The American right was proving to be impenetrable. Pakenham ordered his men to lie still while the artillery reserve was brought forward. He then rode over to his right, where he ordered an officer up a tree with a telescope while he reconnoitered ahead by foot. Pakenham was sure he had found Jackson's weak link. He quickly ordered his artillery to shift from his left to his right flank. While he waited for those cannons that were still functioning, he determined he would need bigger guns and more men if he were to overwhelm the American flank. He ordered a general retreat.

Unfortunately for the shell-shocked British, many of the soldiers would have to wait for nightfall to make their withdrawal. Those farthest from the river and the *Louisiana* made it back to camp first. The left flank came much later. Both flanks, though, suffered the humiliation of retreat. Gleig wrote, "There was not a man among us who failed to experience both shame and indignation, when he found himself retreating before a force for which he entertained the most sovereign contempt."[201]

Naturally, there was jubilation on the other side of Jackson's line. Commodore Patterson boasted to the secretary of the navy of the recent addition of Laffite's Baratarians: "You will have learned from my former letters that the crew of the Louisiana is composed of men of all nations (English excepted) taken from the streets of New Orleans not a fortnight before the battle, yet I never knew guns better served, or a more animated fire, than was supported from her."[202]

Latour had reason to be proud, as the enfilade fire from the *Louisiana*, combined with the batteries perpendicular to the levee road, was decisive in repelling the British reconnaissance. The final casualty tally included seven Americans killed and ten wounded. The British counted sixteen killed and forty-three wounded or missing.[203]

And then there was the crushed psyche of the two hundred Native allies whom Colonel Edward Nicolls had brought to observe the battle. One of the accompanying prophets who had predicted a British victory got "gloriously drunk" that night.[204] Before the reconnaissance, a Cherokee with Nicolls explained to Lieutenant Gleig that "they had come over to the side which they believed to be the strongest, perfectly satisfied that there was no force in Louisiana capable of offering to us any serious resistance."[205]

After a week in the cold and mud, with little progress, Nicolls's allies must have been questioning the wisdom of their decision to support His Britannic Majesty. Surely, a great number of Pakenham's troops were beginning to harbor similar doubts.

37

THE ARTILLERY DUEL

JANUARY 1, 1815

With morale quickly plummeting, Pakenham knew he was running out of time. He *had* to overrun the American breastworks—*soon*. But the reconnaissance had failed to identify any significant weakness.

Pakenham decided he would storm Jackson's line but only after he accomplished two objectives: disable as many American cannons as possible and create a breach in the American earthwork. To do this, he would need bigger guns. Pakenham ordered a number of large-caliber cannons and their corresponding shot to be brought from his ships in the Gulf.

The guns and ammunition were laboriously moved across the Gulf and Lake Borgne, where one boat loaded with cannonballs capsized; its entire crew, each carrying a cannonball in his knapsack, sank to the bottom of the lake as their comrades watched helplessly.[206] The rest of the materiel was moved up Bayou Mazant to within a quarter mile of camp and then laboriously dragged into position.[207]

As he waited for his guns, Pakenham sent Lieutenant Wright—the same man who'd climbed the tree with his telescope three days earlier—to once again reconnoiter the American left. Wright never returned. (His body, still clutching his gun and telescope, was found later. He must have been hit by a stray bullet because his belongings were found on him. Generally, American skirmishers stripped the bodies of British casualties of valuables and weapons.)[208]

Finally, Pakenham's cannons arrived on a wet and rainy New Year's Eve. The general immediately went to work installing his guns within range of Jackson's line.

Line Jackson at Chalmette Battlefield in 2023. *Penelope Starrett.*

Jackson, meanwhile, used the three days following the British reconnaissance to strengthen his own position. Believing that Pakenham would soon receive reinforcements in the form of both men and cannons—and seeing the effectiveness of his own big guns three days before—Jackson added to his own batteries. He placed a thirty-two-pound naval gun (previously aboard the *Carolina*) in his center as well as six-, twelve-, and eighteen-pounders on his left. Commodore Patterson complemented Jackson's line by adding two twelve- and one twenty-four-pounder on the opposite bank, both guns coming from the *Louisiana*. Patterson's addition enabled him to provide a withering enfilade fire on any British troops foolish enough to march down the levee road toward Jackson's line.[209]

With Pakenham adding ten eighteen-pound and four twenty-four-pound cannons to his own arsenal, the arms race alongside Chalmette plantation had reached its zenith.[210]

DESPITE THE RAIN, BRITISH troops worked through the night as quickly and quietly as possible. The rain proved a blessing and a curse. The noise and early morning fog partially hid Pakenham's intentions. Yet the wetness also caused the guns to be mounted in less-than-ideal conditions.

Lieutenant Gleig understood he "worked for life or death"[211] as he and his comrades constructed three redoubts and distributed thirty fieldpieces. Two more howitzers and an oven to heat balls were placed along the levee road, ready to fire on the *Louisiana* should it attempt to join the fray.[212]

Everything was in place for Pakenham by 8:00 a.m. A dense fog limited visibility to twenty yards. After a long, wet night of feverishly preparing their batteries, the British troops waited in grim expectation for the fog to lift.[213]

Silence descended over the battlefield.

The silence did not last long.

Around 9:00 a.m., the fog dissipated, and a thunderous roar broke the eerie, early morning silence as thirty British cannons belched fire and metal toward the American line.[214] Within ten minutes, over one hundred balls, shells, and rockets hit the Macarty house, Jackson's headquarters, which the British believed to be a powder storehouse.

Jackson and his officers were sheltering in the house to strategize, sleep, and escape the rain. They were taken completely by surprise and rushed en masse to the line.[215] After just a few concerted rounds, many of which were fired too high, the British lost the element of surprise. The Americans had exchanged artillery rounds with "the Vanquishers of Napoleon" before.[216] And they had held their ground then. This time, they were prepared and confident.

More Congreve rockets burst through the air, doing little more than alarming the Americans. A few men, however, were struck, one being the wealthy merchant Judah Touro. A fragment of rocket tore through his thigh. So serious was the wound that the doctor who tended him told Reuben Kemper that the wound was likely fatal.[217]

Soon after the first salvos, the American batteries were in action. The motley crew behind Jackson's line had, according to Lieutenant Gleig, "recovered confidence, and answered our salute with great rapidity and precision."[218]

Dominique You, the privateer/pirate who had sailed with Bean from Mexico, was also wounded in the arm by the fragment of a howitzer, causing him to promise his men, "I will pay them for that."[219] A man standing next to Pierre Laffite was instantly killed by a cannonball to the chest.[220] By now, however, the Americans were responding, and their works were far better prepared for an artillery duel than those of the British.

The artillery exchange continued unabated for the next three hours. Each side, alternately, seemed to gain the advantage. A British cannon was disabled. The carriage of Patterson's thirty-two-pounder was damaged.[221] Dominique You and Laffite's Baratarians decommissioned another Redcoat cannon. You's own gun carriage was hit.[222] Barrells of sugar, which had been used to protect the British cannons, exploded in a fiery, sticky rain that coated men and cannons in a viscous adhesive.[223] An American gunboat, loaded with valuable ammunition, was hit and sank to the bottom of the Mississippi River.[224] Yet another British cannon crumbled under the accurate American gunners. Two American caissons were struck, one bursting into volcanic fumes so thunderous and visible that the British artillerymen temporarily ceased firing and cheered the hit. Jackson's line was finally succumbing to superior numbers, experience, and skill.

That strike would signal the high point of the day for His Majesty's troops.

For the next three hours, the combustible remnants of the detonated American caisson burned. Simultaneously, cotton bales, which had been placed to protect the levee battery in front of Plauche's unit, began to burn when a British ball burrowed deep inside. Little damage was done to Jackson's line, but the cotton burned hotter and hotter. Smoke drifted along and in front of Jackson's line as burning shreds of cotton scattered in the wind, a flimsy, gray ash fluttering around the soldiers. The smell of burning cotton, similar to that of burning paper or leaves, permeated the air.[225]

The smell of gunpowder, cotton, and mud surrounded Jackson's line. A damp heat from the weather combined with fifty firing furnaces made the air seem heavy. Smoke, white, gray, and black, covered the land between the armies. Shouting, screaming, and shrieking were occasionally heard over reverberating eardrums. The ground shook, rumbled, and quaked.

And then the three-hour-long crescendo began to slacken.

The British were running out of ammunition.

Pakenham ordered a unit to once again try to turn the American left. The determined British sloshed toward the American flank, but as Arsène Lacarrière-Latour succinctly put it, "Wellington's heroes discovered that they were ill qualified to contend with us in the woods, where they must fight knee deep in water and mud."[226]

Perhaps inevitably, the British flanking movement became mired in the mud, and Pakenham ordered a general withdrawal.

THE DUEL ALONG THE levee continued as Patterson exchanged shots with the British guns along the levee road. The furnace kept the British balls glowing hot and ready to fire on the *Louisiana* should it venture downriver. But Patterson kept his ship out of range. Instead, the British fired on Patterson's works across the river. Latour later reported:

> *The batteries that the enemy had on the river in front of Chalmette's and Bienvenue's houses, continued likewise the whole day to exchange shots with those of Commodore Patterson; and although the balls went through the breastwork, and the shells fell in great numbers in the batteries and on the road, the commodore lost not a single man, nor was his fire for a moment less intense than that of the enemy.*[227]

A cannon behind Line Jackson in 2023. *Joseph Starrett.*

The exchange along the river mirrored the fight along Jackson's line: the British expended most of their balls and shells to little effect. In fact, Patterson suffered not a single casualty. The same could not be said for the British. By noon, all three embankments that held the six batteries were damaged. Several cannons were disabled. Many of the still-functioning guns had been driven deep into the Louisiana mud simply by being fired multiple times.

At noon, the British fire began to slacken. By 3:00 p.m., His Majesty's guns were silenced. Pakenham had conceded. His bombardment had been an utter failure. Gleig confessed, "We were completely foiled."[228] The British army was "not only baffled and disappointed, but in some degree disheartened and discontented."[229]

On the other side, Jackson gloated over the fact that for the second time in five days, he had driven the British back. He wrote to the secretary of war, "Too much praise cannot be bestowed on those who managed my artillery."[230]

Aside from the night attack and a nagging sniper fire, Jackson's muskets and rifles had played only a minor role in the martial tryst.

Soon, they would get their chance to contribute to the engagement.

THAT EVENING, THE MOOD was somber in the British camp. It grew still more morose when Pakenham ordered some of his men to retrieve five abandoned cannons under cover of night. Lieutenant Gleig was one of the unlucky ones chosen for the mission. He would later remember:

> *It was my fortune to accompany them. The labour of dragging a number of huge naval guns out of the soft soil into which they had sunk, crippled, too, as most of them were in their carriages, was more extreme by far than any one expected to find it; indeed, it was not till four o'clock in the morning that our task came to a conclusion, and even then it had been very imperfectly performed.*[231]

Pakenham still had most of his cannons—albeit with a much-reduced supply of shot—and his soldiers (minus the thirty-two killed, forty-four wounded, and two missing that day),[232] but he was running out of time and options.

38

APOTHEOSIS

JANUARY 8, 1815

On January 3, General John Lambert arrived with 2,100 reinforcements, bringing Pakenham's force to little more than 7,000 men.[233] Pakenham, with the input of Admiral Cochrane, devised one final strategy to take the Crescent City. Convinced that he could not outgun the Americans, he decided he would have to take Jackson's line with an old-fashioned frontal assault. Surely, the disciplined British bayonet would carry the day. The militia and dirty shirts would not be able to resist a bold and determined assault. Napoleon hadn't.

Yet Pakenham was also a realist. His plan, therefore, respected what Jackson had been able to accomplish thus far. Pakenham's plan would, in some ways, mimic what his adversary had accomplished two weeks before during the daring night assault. He would divide his army into four units, three of which would attack simultaneously.

The lynchpin would be a 1,400-man force under Colonel William Thornton, which would be rowed across the Mississippi River during the night. Thornton would surprise Patterson and the Americans on the west bank and then take the Marine battery and turn it on Jackson's line across the river. Those same cannons had wreaked havoc on the British left during both the reconnaissance in force and the artillery duel. Now, they would pour an even deadlier fire all along Jackson's right.

With Thornton in command of the west bank and enfilading Jackson's flank, the American general would be forced to shift troops from his left flank to his right, for he would have to deal with not only Thornton but also the second element of Pakenham's plan: General Keane and 1,200 soldiers who would attack down the Levee Road. These men, no longer harassed by Patterson's guns, would storm Jackson's redoubt and then breach the line on Jackson's right.

To assure victory, a third force would assault Jackson's weakened left. This flank, extending into the cypress swamps, had already been proven vulnerable during the reconnaissance and bombardment. Now, with troops rushing to protect the American right, the left would be even more exposed.[234]

General Lambert would be held in reserve with the remaining 1,700 soldiers to expose any impromptu weakness in the American line and to be rested for the final push to New Orleans.

Within twenty-four hours, the hero of Salamanca would either metamorphose into the hero of New Orleans or lose an army—January 8, 1815, would either elevate Pakenham's reputation to that of his famous brother-in-law or cause his name to enter the pantheon of failed American adversaries, joining Generals Howe, Burgoyne, and Cornwallis.[235]

On the same day Lambert arrived with British reinforcements, Jackson, too, received much anticipated reinforcements—2,368 Kentuckians arrived in New Orleans. Yet only 700 brought guns, causing Jackson to fume, "I never in my life seen a Kentuckian without a gun, a pack of cards, and a jug of whiskey."[236]

The frustrated general, who now knew of Lambert's arrival, sent four hundred of the "Kaintucks" to New Orleans to gather whatever muskets and aged weapons they could find and then on to Morgan's line on the west bank. The rest of the unarmed soldiers were sent to rest at Dupre's line, a second line of defense Jackson had constructed a mile behind his primary line. (He had constructed yet a third line another mile and a half behind Dupre's line. If needed, he would be able to retreat and make two additional stands before the British reached New Orleans. If necessary, Jackson planned to sell the city at an exorbitant cost.)[237]

By the time both armies received their reinforcements, Jackson had made much progress on his line. It was a far stronger line than it had been in the days following its construction after the December 23 night attack. And it was stronger since the reconnaissance on December 28 and artillery duel of January 1. In short, Jackson's line was growing stronger by the day. As Pakenham's army weakened in the rainy cold from desertion, disease, and death, the American line only strengthened—hence Pakenham's decision to dare a frontal assault.

Not only had Jackson, per Pierre Laffite's suggestion, lengthened his left flank deeper into the cypress swamp, but he had also added a redoubt directly in front of his right flank (on his side of the Mississippi River). The redoubt was meant to provide enfilade fire as the British approached the main line, to which it was connected by a single plank bridge. However, the ditch around the redoubt was not deep, which caused Jackson to declare, "That will give us trouble!"[238] In the end, Jackson's words regarding the redoubt were both prophetic and irrelevant.

The rest of Jackson's line had been further fortified with additional cannons. By January 7, Jackson had eight batteries supporting thirteen cannons and howitzers along his line.[239]

On the eve of battle, Jackson's line extended 1,650 yards, of which 950 stretched into the cypress swamp and then turned 90 degrees to protect Jackson's flank. That left 700 yards of open field, ideal for a frontal assault—minus the numerous ditches that would have to be traversed and the earthen wall, five feet high at some points and towering over a ditch five to six feet deep, that would have to be stormed, scaled, and taken.[240]

There were also four thousand determined—and now confident—Americans who would have to be dislodged in the process.[241]

Jackson could only hope His Majesty's forces would try his new and improved line. To be sure the attack would come at his front, Jackson sent Reuben Kemper and twenty of his backwoodsmen to keep an eye on the British breastwork at the junction of Bayous Mazant and Bienvenue. Should the British attempt to swing around and behind Jackson's forces, the attempt would germinate there. The British breastwork was well defended, and scouts had climbed the trees to search for any American marauders or spies. In addition, the tall grasses surrounding the position had been burned to prevent any snooping or sneak attack.[242]

These precautions did not matter. Kemper was that good. He and his men kept a careful eye on the position for several days and dutifully reported back to Jackson. The attack would come from Jackson's front against the line he had so carefully prepared.

As doomsday approached, the opposing commanders took stock of the situation: Jackson, confident in the strength of his line and heartened by his men's deportment in the past three engagements; Pakenham, confident in himself, his plan, and the fact that he was British and the Americans were not.

Jackson stared across the field from the Macarty house. Pakenham stared back from a tree he had climbed.[243] Both commanders knew the fate of New Orleans would be decided on the morrow.

Across the river, Commodore Patterson realized the British were going to attack the west bank. The day before, he observed the British digging a canal and immediately realized they were planning to cross the river in force. The west bank was poorly prepared for an attack. Ideally, the *Louisiana* would have simply sailed downriver and made mincemeat of the British transports, but its guns and gunners had been removed to set up Patterson's Marine battery and aid Jackson's line. Additionally, most of the men serving alongside Patterson on the west bank were poorly armed. (Many of the Louisiana militia and the recently arrived Kentuckians carried antiquated muskets and fowling pieces.) And then there were the west bank defenses themselves. Latour, an experienced and talented engineer, had spent most of his resources and energy strengthening Jackson's line. The west bank, by contrast, was buttressed by a weak redoubt. Any reasonably sized British assault would easily overrun both the redoubt and the troops defending it.

Immediately recognizing his peril, Patterson sent a desperate message to Jackson begging for reinforcements. The general was asleep in the Macarty house, aides scattered all along the floor, dressed for battle, swords and pistols nearby. At 1:00 a.m., Patterson's messenger woke Jackson and apprised the general of the situation before making his request, on behalf of Patterson and General Morgan, for reinforcements. Jackson replied, "Hurry back and tell General Morgan that he is mistaken. The main attack will be on this side, and I have no men to spare. He must maintain his position at all hazards."[244] Jackson then woke his aides, saying, "Gentlemen, we have slept enough. Rise. The enemy will be upon us in a few minutes. I must go and see Coffee."[245]

Across the battlefield, Pakenham slept fitfully in the Villere house.

The key to his battle orders was a successful assault on the west bank. But things were not going according to plan. Colonel Thornton was supposed to have landed 1,400 men on the opposite bank, including Gleig's 85th Regiment. To ease Thornton's mission, Admiral Cochrane insisted he could dig a canal across two miles of land to connect Bayou Bienvenue with the Mississippi River. As a result, Thornton's men would be rowed from the bayou to the river with minimal effort.

An exhausted and demoralized army went to work digging a massive canal. Lieutenant Gleig claimed, "[T]he fatigue undergone during the prosecution of this attempt no words can sufficiently describe."[246] Despite the men's round-the-clock fatigue, by January 6, they had completed their Herculean task, but when the dam was broken to release the water needed to carry the barges across, the wet walls of the embankment began to crumble.[247]

The transports then had to be dragged to the Mississippi River. By 3:15 a.m., only 30 boats had made it to the river, carrying 460 men. Thornton himself still awaited transport. It was clear he would not be able to turn Patterson's cannons and support the main attack.

Events on Pakenham's side of the river were hardly going better, though the general could not have realized it at the time.

The night before battle, Pakenham ordered Colonel Thomas Mullins of the 44th Regiment to make sure the fascines and ladders necessary to scale the walls above the ditch—as high as a dozen feet in some places—were in place, for without them, the wall on the American left could not be scaled. The ineffectiveness of the British cannons made the ladders and fascines indispensable. There would be no way to scale the American defenses without them. Instead, the British troops would be mired down beneath the earthwork at the mercy of American riflemen. Mullins was explicitly ordered: "The advance guard is to carry forward with it, six long ladders with planks on them and ten small ladders as well as the fascines. The commanding officer of the 44th Regiment must ascertain where these requisites are, this evening, so that there will be no delay in taking them forward tomorrow to the old batteries."[248]

Mullins sent an aide to determine the exact location of the essential materiel. Rather than confirming the location himself, Mullins heard from several officers that the fascines and ladders were at the advance redoubt and advance battery. Assuming the two were synonymous, Mullins trusted he would find the equipment on his way to the front in the morning.

He learned in the morning that the advance redoubt and advance battery were half a mile apart.[249]

At 5:00 a.m., Pakenham woke and immediately rode to check on the progress on the west bank. The news was not good. Only a portion of Thornton's troops had made the crossing, the colonel joining the last departures. Those who made it to the opposite bank arrived one thousand yards downstream. A coordinated attack along both banks was no longer possible.[250]

Pakenham faced an agonizing choice: call off the attack and suffer more casualties via disease and desertion or proceed with a frontal assault and suffer untold casualties via ball and bullet. On the one hand, his troops were hungry, cold, demoralized, and itching for a fight. On the other, Jackson's line was growing stronger with each passing day.

Pakenham chose to proceed with the attack.

Lieutenant Colonel Robert Dale of the 93rd Highlanders took off his watch and handed it, along with a letter to his wife, to his physician, saying, "Give these to my wife; I shall die at the head of my regiment."[251] Colonel Mullins was equally prescient. The night before, he had exclaimed, "My regiment has been ordered to execution! Their dead bodies are to be used as a bridge for the rest of the army to march over!"[252]

At 4:00 a.m., General John Adair marched his one-thousand-man reinforcement to a place fifty yards behind Carrol's unit. Adair's placement, by fortunate coincidence, happened to be at just the spot where Britain's most dangerous thrust would occur. The American troops ate a hot breakfast and drank hotter coffee. (Throughout the two-week ordeal, American troops had been dining on rations of beef or pork, bread, whiskey, and coffee, plus whatever they could buy from local traveling vendors at prices that were kept low as a result of the British blockade, which had caused food to pile up in New Orleans warehouses.) The British, on the other hand, subsisted on salted meat, hard biscuits, and grog.[253] By the morning of battle, the latter meager, flavorless, and redundant rations had been reduced to dry biscuits, as the British troops had not been allowed to light fires on the eve of battle.[254] Cold, miserable, and hungry, His Majesty's troops eagerly awaited the dawn, an assault, and the end to their misery.

With the odds stacked against him, Pakenham still had time to call off the assault.

He did not.

Just before sunrise, a signal rocket screeched through the air, visible from Pakenham's line of battle, Jackson's line, and the west bank.

The final act of the Battle of New Orleans had commenced.

WITH THE FIRING OF the rocket, the British opened a deafening barrage on the American line, breaking the silence of the dawn. By now, the mist had begun to lift, and each side could see two hundred to three hundred yards ahead of them. The Americans promptly answered with their own salvo, so deadly and accurate that Lieutenant Gleig would later recall, "[The Americans] opened upon us from right to left, a fire of musketry, grape, round-shot, and canister, than which I have certainly never witnessed any more murderous."[255] Cannon smoke, mingling with the fading mist, further obscured the field, but on each side, bursts of flame at the cannons' mouths gave away their location as the guns spewed forth their deadly projectiles.

As the cannons roared, the British army began their final march toward Jackson's line, a march that was destined to see them capture the Crescent City—or many hundreds, perhaps thousands, die in the attempt.

Unlike Jackson's four-pronged night attack two weeks prior, Pakenham's January 8 attack was anything but coordinated. Historian Robert V. Remini claims, "Pakenham's impetuosity in the Peninsular War had brought victory. Here outside New Orleans it would bring devastating defeat."[256]

Colonel Thornton was a nonfactor on the west bank.

Just as disastrous, Colonel Mullins never delivered the ladders and fascines to the British right. The night before, he had been told the necessary materiel were in an advanced redoubt. Mullins never confirmed the assertion.[257] Now, with the assault underway, Mullins realized his mistake. He immediately sent 300 of his 427 men back to retrieve the ladders and fascines. By the time they returned, all was chaos at the front. Mullins's 44th advanced, carrying the ladders and fascines, but with little covering fire from their own side and deadly fusillades erupting from the American line, most of the ladder bearers dropped their loads and began returning fire.

The ladders and fascines never made it to the line.[258]

Many of Pakenham's soldiers on his right flank, under General Gibbs, did, but without the scaling ladders, they were doomed.

Pakenham began the battle commanding from the center. Both his flanks, under Gibbs and Keane, advanced. Suddenly, Pakenham made an impromptu and fateful decision. He galloped forward and ordered the 93rd Highlanders, who had been supporting Keane's assault on the American right, to cut diagonally across the field to support Gibbs's assault on the American left. Pakenham must have assumed that with no Thornton turning the American guns on the west bank, those same guns would be used to rake the British left. With both Jackson and Patterson focused on Pakenham's left, the 93rd would have an easier time on the other flank, especially with the ladders and fascines now in place.[259]

Only they weren't.

Ironically, General Keane had already made inroads against the American right. Colonel Robert Rennie stormed and took the American redoubt and began spiking the guns. Yet Rennie's bold charge proved a suicide mission, for just as he took the redoubt, the 93rd was ordered on their own ill-fated march toward the opposite flank. Rennie was left alone.

Unfazed—or perhaps ignorant of his situation—Rennie leapt from the redoubt to Jackson's line, urging his men on and promising them, "The day is ours!" The courageous Rennie ran into the first cannon embrasure. One of Beale's riflemen awaited him and promptly shot him through the left eye. The ball entered Rennie's brain, killing him just as another defender thrust his pike into the colonel's body.[260] Every British soldier who entered the redoubt was either killed or captured.[261]

With his focus now on his right flank, Pakenham quickly ascertained that the attack was beginning to unravel. He galloped toward what he believed was the critical sector of the battlefield. As he rode amid the carnage, he saw Mullins's 44th fleeing. "Lost for want of courage!" he yelled to an aide. To the stalled 93rd, he promised, "93rd, have a little patience, and you shall soon have your revenge!"[262]

Seeing his attack thwarted, General Gibbs rode toward the front. Along the way, he encountered Mullins and exclaimed, "Colonel Mullins, if I live till tomorrow, you shall be hanged from one of these trees!"

Gibbs never fulfilled his threat. He was shot dead moments later, the first of the British leadership that day to succumb to American sharpshooters.

With no orders to retreat and no ladders that would enable them to advance, the 93rd halted and took devastating fire from Jackson's line. A frustrated Pakenham rode to rally his right. Grapeshot tore through his leg and killed his horse. His aide-de-camp, Duncan Macdougal, leapt from his own horse and helped his general to his feet. (He had done the same for General Ross outside Baltimore, only Ross's wound proved mortal.) In what must have been a moment of déjà vu, Macdougal's commander-in-chief was then shot in the arm. Still, Pakenham moved forward. Macdougal helped him mount his own horse and led his general onward.

Again, Pakenham was shot, this time falling from the borrowed horse and into the arms of Macdougal.[263]

The hero of Salamanca would not arise again.

The death of General Edward Pakenham only delayed the inevitable. In effect, the battle was over when the general ordered the signal flare fired into the air earlier that morning.

General Keane was shot in the groin, ending the assault on the left. With the top three commanders dead, dying, and near dying, General Lambert, now the ranking commander on the field, ordered a general retreat.

The fight on the west bank was a marked contrast to what occurred in front of Jackson's line.

General Morgan had sent 120 poorly armed men to a position three miles south of his camp to keep an eye on British movements and deter them if they crossed the river. Even though Thornton was eight hours behind schedule and had been carried half a mile downstream by the powerful Mississippi River, he was able to affect a complete surprise, overrunning the American advance position with ease. Thornton's double-quick march was so bold and disciplined that he nearly captured the stunned Louisiana militiamen, who promptly fled.[264]

Thornton marched on, hot in pursuit. Only when he was within seven hundred yards of Morgan's main line did he order his men to halt so he could reconnoiter Morgan's position. He immediately realized Morgan's defense had a glaring weakness along the British left, three hundred yards from the Mississippi River. Thornton ordered a general assault on the line to keep the Americans spread thin. The main thrust of his assault, however, smashed the American right and quickly turned the flank.

The battle on the left bank was as one-sided as its counterpart on the right.

Commodore Patterson had been firing across the river all morning, enfilading the British main assault. Now, with Morgan's troops in a panicked retreat and Thornton bearing down on him, he had time to neither turn his guns nor spike all of them. His battery would soon be at the bottom of the Mississippi River or in the hands of the British.

Patterson did what damage he could to his own guns and then cursed the Kentuckians for fleeing the line (he even considered firing a cannon on those he deemed cowards) and then cursed the British before he calmly led his men north toward the *Louisiana*. He was able to move his last boat out of range of the British guns, but his batteries were of no more use to Jackson.

The battle had been a complete success for Thornton. And yet he immediately ascertained it was a pyrrhic victory when he gazed across the great river and saw the one-sided carnage.

On his own bank, Thornton lost six men, with another seventy-six wounded, including himself. The Americans had lost only one dead and three wounded, but another thirty had been captured, along with fifteen cannons and a howitzer.[265] Even more devastating to the American cause, the British now controlled Jackson's right flank. Thornton had placed the British in a prime position to continue the battle.[266]

A deeply concerned Jackson sent Pierre Laffite across the river to advise Morgan how he could best utilize the canals and terrain to his advantage. It was imperative that the British be driven from his flank. Once Morgan heard Laffite's advice, he sent the smuggler back across the river to request reinforcements. He asked that Laffite return as quickly as possible to help familiarize him with the terrain. Jackson, in turn, sent Laffite back with a promise of reinforcements to come that evening.[267]

Only now, General Lambert had had enough. He sent word to Thornton to call off the attack and rejoin the British units across the river to help repel a potential American counterattack.

In a masterful and daring retreat, the remainder of Thornton's outfit was able to recross the river they had crossed earlier that morning, adding the only victorious arm of the British army to Lambert's decimated command.

The Battle of New Orleans was effectively over.

Around noon, a British trumpeter and soldier carrying a white flag marched across the field of battle and stopped three hundred yards from Jackson's line. The former blared some notes while the latter waved his flag. Jackson sent three officers to meet with the defeated British. They delivered a note from Lambert that asked for a ceasefire to treat the wounded strewn across Chalmette plantation and gather the dead.

After a string of exchanged letters, in which Jackson learned that the British high command had been wiped out and Lambert was now in charge, the American general granted generous conditions for the retrieval of his enemy's wounded. But first, at the vehement request of Commodore Patterson, the general insisted that he learn the fate and condition of those sailors captured on Lake Borgne on December 14. Lambert complied, and the negotiation proceeded. Not wanting the British to get close enough to gather intelligence on his line, Jackson promised to take care of all British soldiers within the immediate vicinity of his defenses. The British would be given until 2:00 p.m. the following day to gather the rest.[268]

If erecting the initial batteries or digging the futile canal had been a Herculean task, retrieving the dead and materiel scattered over the battlefield was worse. Only now, His Majesty's forces were no longer working toward a victory but salvaging what they could after an undeniable and disastrous defeat. Many of the men they carried back to hospitals and graveyards were their companions and close friends.

And the British had a whole lot of companions and close friends to move. The casualty discrepancy was astonishing. During the January 8 assault, the Americans lost 7 killed and 6 wounded. The British reported 291 killed, 1,262 wounded, and 484 captured.[269]

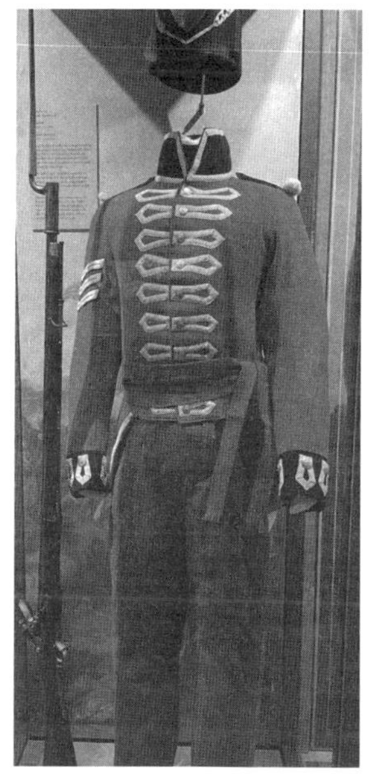

British uniforms from the Chalmette Battlefield and National Cemetery Visitor Center. *Ryan Starrett.*

The field itself was dyed red, both metaphorically and literally. Red-coated soldiers lay everywhere. Jackson wrote on the following day, January 9, "[U]pwards of 300 of the dead were picked up by my troops, and delivered over to the enemy for burial. We took about 500 prisoners; the greater part of whom were dangerously and many of them mortally wounded."[270]

The dead, both those handed over by Jackson and those retrieved by the British, were buried on Bienvenue's plantation. (Many of the deceased were carried to their grave on the scaling ladders that had been left on the field of battle.)[271] The wounded were taken to La Ronde's home, where every room was quickly filled, and the amputations continued through the night. General Keane lay suffering in the same room where Pakenham and Gibbs's corpses were awaiting disembowelment so they could be preserved in a cask of rum for burial in their homelands across the sea.[272] It was expected that Keane would soon join Pakenham

Battle of New Orleans, by Kurz and Allison (1890). *Library of Congress.*

and Gibbs in death. However, when the bullet passed through the general's pants and underwear, it pulled the fabric into Keane's thigh. A surgeon was able to gently pull the fabric out, and the bullet came with it. Keane would outlive his commanding general by twenty-nine years.[273] The survivors camped out in the cold, listening to the sawing and the screaming.[274]

Even those who did survive the battle intact left vivid images in the minds of those who watched from Jackson's line. Hundreds of soldiers lay silently among the dead until the firing was over. When it was safe, these men began to rise alone and in groups. Some sprinted for the safety of British lines; others marched like defeated ghosts, arms raised, toward the American defenses. Jackson would later comment, "I never had so grand and awful an idea of the resurrection as on that day."[275]

Lieutenant Gleig stared at the field from the opposite side. His reflection juxtaposes the jubilant mood of the Americans:

> *Parties were immediately sent out to collect and bury their fallen comrades. Prompted by curiosity, I mounted my horse, and rode to the front; but of all the sights I ever witnessed, that which met me there was beyond comparison the most shocking, and the most humiliating. Within the small compass of a few hundred yards, were gathered together nearly a thousand bodies, all of them arrayed in British uniforms. Not a single American was among them; all were English; and they were thrown by dozens into shallow holes, scarcely deep enough to furnish them with a slight covering of earth....I confess that when I beheld the scene, I hung down my head half in sorrow, half in anger....I turned my horse's head and galloped back to the camp.*[276]

The Battle of New Orleans, thus far, had been an unmitigated triumph for the Americans and a disaster for the British.

But Jackson was not yet satisfied.

And the British had not yet surrendered the dream of "beauty and booty."

39
THE RETREAT
JANUARY 9–27, 1815

Jackson considered following up the British assault of January 8 with a counterattack of his own. He dearly hoped for a final blow that would turn a decisive victory into an utter annihilation. Jackson's advisors, however, convinced him not to give the British the advantage they had just given him: the gift of defending a narrow field from a defensive position. The general accepted this sound advice, but he was determined to kill, capture, and harass as many Redcoats as he could. The bombardment would continue night and day and so would the nighttime "hunting parties" of his dirty shirts. Jackson was convinced that if he kept the enemy bogged down, eventually, bullets, weather, and desertions would lead to their utter ruin.

Patterson's shells did their job—so did Kemper and the other night hunters. British Captain Henry Cooke would later recall the burial of a fellow officer who succumbed to his January 8 wounds. "The night after this burial a shell exploded over a hut in which two officers of our regiment were sleeping, which cut off the feet of Lieutenant D'Arcy. One of his feet was driven so deep into the soft [mud] that it was obliged to be dug out the following day."[277]

Lieutenant Gleig recorded his own traumatic memories of those last two and a half weeks outside New Orleans:

> *We never closed our eyes in peace. Tents we had none and heavy rains now set in, accompanied by violent storms of thunder and lightning which, lasting during the entire day usually ceased towards dark and gave place*

> *to keen frosts. Thus were we alternately wet and frozen. The outposts* [pickets] *were attacked and compelled to maintain their ground by dint of hard fighting.*[278]

Despite the defeat of January 8, Admiral Cochrane had not yet given up his dream of plunder and conquest. The morning of January 8, he had sent five boats up the Mississippi River with the intention of pounding Fort St. Philip into submission. If Cochrane could take this American outpost eighty miles south of New Orleans and then overrun the hopelessly weak American defenses at English Turn, Cochrane could then enfilade Jackson's troops and, with control of the entire Mississippi, land an army behind the American line.

Cochrane's plan, just like the plan on the West Bank, was solid. Unlike events on the West Bank, however, the attack on Fort St. Philip was an unmitigated failure. After nine days of bombarding the fort and firing seventy tons' worth of shells, the British had killed only two Americans. Worse, Fort St. Philip was still returning fire. Worse still, with each passing day, Lambert's position became even more untenable and dangerous. On January 18, Cochrane called off the attack.[279]

Despite Cochrane's bluster, Lambert could see the writing on the wall. On January 9, he began putting in motion the inevitable retreat. He had two major obstacles. The path his army had taken back on December 22 was even swampier and muddier after two and a half weeks of wet, wintry weather. The march back would be a slog through the ninth circle of hell. Worse, there weren't enough boats to move even half of his army to safety. The other half would be left at the mercy of the Americans.

Lambert focused on what he could control and began constructing a road from his camp to the bayou. It took eight days to complete. Then under cover of darkness and in utter silence, his men began to withdraw. The march to Lake Borgne was even worse than he anticipated. As each unit slogged through the marsh, the road worsened. Soldiers marched up to their ankles in muck. Those behind were buried up to their calves. Then knees. And thighs.

Some never made it to the bank. Lieutenant Gleig saw a soldier ahead of him sink up to his chest and then continue sinking. He tried to help his comrade, only to begin sinking himself. His companion soon disappeared entirely into the swamp. At that moment, a more prudent soldier tossed Gleig a canteen strap, and the fortunate lieutenant was saved from a claustrophobic, suffocating death.[280]

Eventually, the army made it to the edge of the lake. Now, the frigid sailors went to work rowing the units piecemeal out to the fleet. Those ashore waited for the increasingly exhausted sailors to make the sixty-mile trip over turbulent water to return and gather another unit. And another.

Those left ashore, waiting, were told to make themselves comfortable. There was much laughter. Hours passed, then days. The food was gone. An expert shot, Gleig shot a duck. It fell twenty yards into the water, the edge coated in ice—so did the next four ducks. His dog refused to enter the frigid water. The dog's starving master plunged in. A few hours later, a bone-chilled Gleig enjoyed perhaps his most delectable meal to date.[281]

Finally, on January 27, the last of the British survivors rejoined the British fleet.

ANDREW JACKSON, STILL CONVINCED that Britain would renew its assault on New Orleans, kept martial law in effect and began frantically reinforcing all possible approaches to the city. He was convinced the campaign was not over and was as determined as ever to keep the British at sea.

Arsène Lacarrière-Latour, as one of Jackson's two chief engineers, had plenty of work to do in strengthening the various American defenses over the next month. Ever observant, the engineer cast a keen eye on his surroundings and an open ear toward the battle's participants.

Peter Ellis Bean, having successfully driven an imperial foe from his native land, continued to recruit and seek material aid from his new comrades in arms. He hoped to gain support for his fellow revolutionaries west and south of the border.

Reuben Kemper, always itching for a fight with foreigners on his native soil, scouted for Jackson and continued to seek out British soldiers who might fall within range of his guns.

Pierre Laffite, with his eyes on the battlefield but also the future, stayed by Jackson's side, offering advice and poring over maps of the region. His loyalty and hard work ensured the pardon Jackson had promised. And after that? He and Jean would rebuild their empire.

Commodore Patterson, having lost most of his flotilla, redeemed himself at his land batteries, and he had his work cut out in the future. With the British now at sea, another amphibious assault—somewhere—was most likely. Even if he had only the *Louisiana* at his present disposal, he would soon be called to put his experience and expertise with coastal batteries to use—somewhere.

Edward Nicolls, angry at the British performance and embarrassed on behalf of the Natives he had brought with promises of a glorious spectacle, began reassessing his role on the Gulf Coast. Having seen his hopes for a British-controlled coast evaporate, what would happen to the Black men and Natives he had induced, in good faith, to join his crusade?

George Robert Gleig, having experienced a year few soldiers ever do—in which he fought on two continents, exiled an emperor, burned an enemy capital, partook in the birth of a national anthem, sailed the Caribbean, and nearly met his end multiple times in a swamp eight miles outside the United States' most exotic city—kept his observations to himself. Later, he would share them with the world.

Edward Pakenham, no longer anxious over tactics and strategy, no longer cursed with broken sleep and fitful dreams, no longer filled with apprehension and concern, lay disemboweled and stuffed in a cask of rum.

40

THE END

JANUARY 28–FEBRUARY 13, 1815

The end of the War of 1812 came abruptly. Between February 8 and 11, Admiral Cochrane, as Andrew Jackson feared and suspected, opened a new front with the capture of Fort Bowyer. Mobile was now exposed. A far easier path toward New Orleans lay open. Jackson and company would now likely have to fight the British from a far-less-advantageous position than they had at Chalmette, very possibly pitting American militia against British regulars in the open, just as they had at Bladensburg.

Two days later, the British learned that their victory at Fort Bowyer (and defeat at New Orleans) had been in vain.

The final treaty, the Treaty of Ghent, which suspended fighting under the principal of status quo ante bellum ("the state of affairs that existed before the war"), was sent to the United States Congress. (Britain had already ratified the treaty on December 30, two days before the artillery duel at Chalmette.) At the United States' ratification of the treaty, the War of 1812 ended.[282]

In the end, the Battle of New Orleans had been for naught.

Or had it?

Aside from the 2,767 casualties from both sides, mostly British—many of whom would never return home, progenerate, or contribute, positively or negatively, to the world around them—the battle cemented the newly formed United States as a world player. Still nascent and aspiring, the young country was now destined to determine the fate of the North American continent, especially with men like Peter Ellis Bean and Reuben Kemper aiding in the dissolution of the Spanish empire. Soon after, largely due to the efforts of Jackson, Pensacola and St. Augustine fell into the American orbit. A decade and a half later, Texas would break away and then join the United States. The Monroe Doctrine was in effect. The principle of Manifest Destiny was gaining steam—and to Edward Nicolls's chagrin, so was the expansion of slavery.

And then came the Civil War. Cuba. Puerto Rico. Empire. The decisive intervention in World War I. World War II. The civil rights movement (the Second/Third American Revolutions). The leader of the free world, a world inspired and dominated by American policy.

But without the pivotal Battle of New Orleans?

Britain never accepted the Louisiana Purchase. Had they conquered New Orleans, would the entire Gulf Coast *Game of Thrones*–esque cycle have been altered? Would New Orleans have been ceded to Britain's ambivalent/Anglophilic/Anglophobic/sometimes ally Spain? Would the principle of status quo antebellum have extended to the Creeks and would Nicolls's fort for Native and Black refugees been adequately defended?

One way or another, the goals, dreams, ambitions, failures, nightmares, and triumphs of those on the waters and fields between the Mississippi Sound and Jackson's line mattered. Nearly three thousand either never left the field of battle or carried reminders of the fight for the rest of their days. More than ten thousand others reveled in and suffered from the aftermath of the battle, as soldiers from time immemorial have. Each soldier brings their own story to the battlefield, and many live their own stories afterward. It was no different for the men who took their own various roads to New Orleans in 1814.

This book tells just nine of those stories.

EPILOGUE

Edward Nicolls

Nicolls inwardly raged at the defeat outside New Orleans. He had promised much to many, and now his word and his ideals were in jeopardy. As a military man, Nicolls understood orders. He would have to abandon the maroon colony he had worked so honestly and diligently to establish. Before doing so, he negotiated a treaty in which the Red Stick Creeks would pledge allegiance to Britain and, in return, be protected as British subjects. To his disgust, the treaty would not be ratified by Britain, and within a year and a half, most of his former recruits were killed, captured, or on the run. Nevertheless, Nicolls went on to serve Great Britain for another forty years, most proudly off the African coast in his country's attempt to abolish the slave trade.

George Robert Gleig

After leaving the bloodied plantations outside New Orleans and the long wait on Dauphin Island, Gleig finally boarded a ship for England. On his arrival, he learned that Napoleon was back. Europe was once again convulsed by war—but this time for only one hundred days. Once peace was reestablished,

Gleig finished his studies and spent the rest of his life balancing clerical and martial duties, as well as writing extensively. The memoir of his adventures during the War of 1812 and, most notably, the Battle of New Orleans is an indispensable source for students and aficionados of the climactic battle of the war.

EDWARD PAKENHAM

Of the nine characters who inspired this book, Pakenham is the only one who did not survive the battle. He was never able to explain his actions, redeem his reputation, or atone for his colossal failure. Pakenham, however, would be remembered as a gallant hero. Given a daunting hand, Pakenham did not have the humility and fortitude to withdraw. And still, had things gone right on the night of January 7, most notably with Thornton's river crossing and Mullins's fascines and ladders, Pakenham might have pulled off a most improbable victory. Instead, his body was packed in a cask of rum and returned to Ireland, where he was laid to rest in his family's vault. Great Britain honored Pakenham, along with his fellow fallen General Gibbs, with a statue, which still stands outside St. Paul's Cathedral in London today.

JEAN AND PIERRE LAFFITE

The brothers Laffite were immediately pardoned in lieu of their service at the Battle of New Orleans. Their celebrity shone brighter than ever in the city—but for only a short while. With American supremacy on the Gulf assured and extended, the days of privateering and smuggling were numbered. Within four years, the brothers were on the run and, oddly, at odds with the nation they had so recently backed. The brothers reestablished their destroyed Baratarian base in Galveston, only to be forced out by the United States in 1820. One year later, Pierre, wounded by Spanish troops and suffering from a severe fever, died in the arms of his then-current lover on the Yucatan Peninsula. Jean was killed two years later while attacking a Spanish brigantine.

PETER ELLIS BEAN

Bean left the United States disappointed. He had helped his native land resist a colonial power, only to have his country refuse to aid his adopted homeland in its struggle for independence against a colonial power. Nevertheless, Bean returned to Mexico and spent the next three decades vacillating between residences in Mexico and the United States—and between his Mexican and American wives. Bean's military career even extended to the Texas Revolution, where his loyalties were more conflicted than ever. After Texas won its independence, he chose to live in Nacogdoches, Texas, but soon after migrated back to Veracruz, Mexico, where the perpetually rambling revolutionary finally ended his wanderings in 1846.

REUBEN KEMPER

After helping expel two foreign empires from his lands and along the Gulf Coast, Kemper retired to a relatively uneventful life. He spent the next dozen years working his land and died in Natchez in 1827. Before his death, Kemper saw all his dreams come to fruition: the Stars and Stripes flew over Baton Rouge, Mobile, and St. Augustine; the Spanish were driven entirely from the coast; and the United States was making inroads into Mexican Texas. Kemper, no longer a border ruffian but a regional, if not national, hero, died peacefully at home and was buried with military honors in the Natchez City Cemetery.

ARSÈNE LACARRIÈRE-LATOUR

A year after the Battle of New Orleans, Latour published his memoir of the climactic battle. It is still considered one of the finest primary sources of the battle and campaign. Latour used his celebrity to mingle with an eclectic group, including U.S. presidents, foreign agents, and filibusters. Latour remains a man of mystery, with prominent scholars either unsure or divided about where his loyalties lay—to Spain or the United States. One thing is certain: Latour, despite any potential side income, continued to earn his living as a talented urban planner and engineer, the same skills that had earned him the gratitude of a nation.

DANIEL TODD PATTERSON

A consummate Navy man, Patterson remained in the service until his death twenty-five years after the Battle of New Orleans. A grateful Andrew Jackson praised his service throughout the Battle of New Orleans, and Congress awarded him by making him the captain and commander of the USS *Constitution*. Patterson spent the rest of his career and life sailing the Mediterranean Sea and overseeing the Washington Navy Yard. The United States Navy has named three ships after Patterson.

ANDREW JACKSON

Jackson rode the momentum of the Battle of New Orleans all the way to the White House fourteen years later. In between, he feuded with the New Orleans Creole aristocracy and government over his continuance of martial law after the British abandoned the city's environs. The hero of New Orleans was even summoned and fined for contempt of court. Despite many who were willing to pay his expenses, Jackson paid his own fine. The animosity between the city and Jackson ended on the twenty-fifth anniversary of the battle, when the former general and president returned to the city that had made him a household name. In 1851, New Orleans erected a statue of the general and renamed the Place d'Armes Jackson Square in his honor.

NOTES

Chapter 1

1. Patterson, *Generals*, 7.
2. Patterson, *Generals*, 7–8.
3. Patterson, *Generals*, 10.
4. Groom, *Patriotic Fire*, 37.

Chapter 2

5. Bean, *Memoir*, 6–7.
6. Bean, *Memoir*, 8.
7. Bean, *Memoir*, 11.
8. Bean, *Memoir*, 12.

Chapter 3

9. Garrigoux, *Visionary Adventurer*, 24.
10. Garrigoux, *Visionary Adventurer*, 27.
11. Garrigoux, *Visionary Adventurer*, 49.
12. Garrigoux, *Visionary Adventurer*, 52.
13. Garrigoux, *Visionary Adventurer*, 53.
14. Garrigoux, *Visionary Adventurer*, 55.
15. Garrigoux, *Visionary Adventurer*, 56.
16. Garrigoux, *Visionary Adventurer*, 56.

Chapter 4

17. Davis, *Rogue Republic*, 7–12.
18. Davis, *Rogue Republic*, 12–13.
19. Davis, *Rogue Republic*, 22.
20. Davis, *Rogue Republic*, 22.
21. Davis, *Rogue Republic*, 25.
22. Davis, *Rogue Republic*, 27.
23. Davis, *Rogue Republic*, 41–42.

Chapter 5

24. Bainbridge earlier surrendered the schooner *Retaliation* to the French during the Quasi War in 1798 and was later forced by the Dey of Algeria to use his frigate USS *George Washington* to carry gifts and bribes to Constantinople. The ship was also forced to fly the Algerian flag during the humiliating mission.
25. Kilmeade and Yaeger, *Thomas Jefferson*, 122–24.
26. Kilmeade and Yaeger, *Thomas Jefferson*, 125–26.
27. Kilmeade and Yaeger, *Thomas Jefferson*, 126.
28. Vallar, "Scottish Pirates."
29. Kilmeade and Yaeger, *Thomas Jefferson*, 127.
30. Kilmeade and Yaeger, *Thomas Jefferson*, 125.
31. Kilmeade and Yaeger, *Thomas Jefferson*, 148–49.
32. Kilmeade and Yaeger, *Thomas Jefferson*, 194.
33. Kilmeade and Yaeger, *Thomas Jefferson*, 193.
34. Naval History and Heritage Command, "Daniel Todd Patterson."

Chapter 6

35. Davis, *Rogue Republic*, 69–70.
36. Davis, *Rogue Republic*, 71–72.
37. Davis, *Rogue Republic*, 72–73.
38. Davis, *Rogue Republic*, 74.
39. Davis, *Rogue Republic*, 75.

Chapter 7

40. Bean, *Memoir*, 14.
41. Bean, *Memoir*, 17–19.

42. Bean, *Memoir*, 21–24.
43. Bean, *Memoir*, 26.

Chapter 8

44. France regained a number of its islands in the aftermath of the Napoleonic Wars. As of 2025, St. Martin, Guadalupe, Martinique, and Saint-Barthelemy are part of France.
45. Three Decks, "Capture of St. Lucia and Tobago, 21st June 1803," www.threedecks.org; Patterson, *Generals*, 27–28.
46. Patterson, *Generals*, 30–31. The Battle of Martinique was orchestrated by Admiral Alexander Cochrane, who would have much to do with the Battle of New Orleans five years later. Cochrane helped plan the initial invasion. Pakenham was left to salvage what he could from the mess Cochrane left him.
47. Grocott, *Shipwrecks*, 326–28.

Chapter 9

48. Bean, *Memoir*, 27.
49. Bean, *Memoir*, 29–33.

Chapter 10

50. Davis, *Rogue Republic*, 114–15.

Chapter 11

51. Thomas Hobbes.
52. Saxon, *Fabulous New Orleans*, 163.
53. Foreman, "History."

Chapter 12

54. For administrative purposes, Florida was divided into two parts. West Florida was governed from Pensacola and extended from the Apalachicola River to Natchez and Baton Rouge, while East Florida extended to the Atlantic Ocean and was governed from St. Augustine.
55. Davis, *Rogue Republic*, 203.

56. Davis, *Rogue Republic*, 217.
57. Davis, *Rogue Republic*, 231.
58. Davis, *Rogue Republic*, 233–34.
59. Davis, *Rogue Republic*, 235.
60. Davis, *Rogue Republic*, 262.
61. "The Eyes of the Nation Will Be Diverted," *Alexandria Gazette*, May 29, 1813.

Chapter 13

62. Patterson, *Generals*, 77.
63. Patterson, *Generals*, 78.
64. Patterson, *Generals*, 78.

Chapter 14

65. Patterson, *Generals*, 81.
66. Patterson, *Generals*, 84. A summary of the Battle of Salamanca can be found on these pages of Patterson's work.
67. In another of history's ironies, Pakenham met his fate on a field outside New Orleans—the same city that would, allegedly, offer Napoleon refuge should he escape exile a second time (John R. Kemp, "1905," *New Orleans*, March 1, 2022, www.myneworleans.com).

Chapter 15

68. Davis, *Pirates Laffite*, 90–91.
69. Davis, *Pirates Laffite*, 91–95.
70. Davis, *Pirates Laffite*, 116.
71. A heavy line was attached from boat to shore, and the boat was hauled upstream by either men or animals on shore.
72. Davis, *Pirates Laffite*, 118–22.
73. Davis, *Pirates Laffite*, 122.
74. Davis, *Pirates Laffite*, 122–23.

Chapter 16

75. The title of this chapter is taken from Tony Turnbow's history of Jackson's 1813 march down and back up the Natchez Trace (Turnbow, *Hardened to Hickory*).
76. Turnbow, *Hardened to Hickory*, 340.

77. Turnbow, *Hardened to Hickory*, 368.
78. Turnbow, *Hardened to Hickory*, 387.
79. Turnbow, *Hardened to Hickory*, 397.
80. Turnbow, *Hardened to Hickory*, 411.

Chapter 17

81. Music-And-Art-45, "3 Famous Duels Involving Andrew Jackson," Owlcation, November 20, 2023, www.owlcation.com.
82. "Do you bite your thumb at us, sir?" "No, sir, I do not bite my thumb at you, sir, but I bite my thumb, sir."
83. The younger Benton's pistol was loaded with two balls and a slug. The slug shattered Jackson's shoulder while one of the balls lodged in his arm (Patterson, *Generals*, 102).
84. This vignette can be found in Elbert B. Smith, "Now Defend Yourself, You Damned Rascal!," *American Heritage* 2, no. 2 (February 1958), www.americanheritage.com; Patterson, *Generals*, 102–3.

Chapter 18

85. Davis, *Greatest Fury*, 16.
86. Obituary, *Daily Universal Register*, February 9, 1865, 12; "General Nicolls," *Gentleman's Magazine and Historical Review*, 644–46.

Chapter 19

87. Patterson, *Generals*, 179; U.S. Customs and Border Protection, "John Stout," www.cbp.gov.
88. *Shannon Selin*, "Pirate Consorts: Marie and Catherine Villard," www.shannonselin.com.
89. Davis, *Pirates Lafitte*, 158.
90. Davis, *Pirates Lafitte*, 158.
91. Davis, *Pirates Lafitte*, 160.
92. Davis, *Pirates Lafitte*, 161.

Chapter 20

93. American Battlefield Trust, "Alexander Cochrane: Proclamation A British Appeal to American Slaves: Bermuda, April 2,1814," www.battlefields.org.
94. Owsley, *Struggle*, 103.
95. Davis, *Greatest Fury*, 17.
96. Davis, *Greatest Fury*, 18.

Chapter 21

97. U.S. Environmental Protection Agency, "The Mississippi/Atchafalaya River Basin (MARB)," www.epa.gov.
98. Gleig, *Campaigns of the British Army*, 65–66.
99. Gleig, *Campaigns of the British Army*, 68.
100. The accounts of the Battle of Bladensburg and the burning of Washington, D.C., can be found in Gleig's memoir and the following webpages: American Battlefield Trust, "Bladensburg," www.battlefields.org; and American Battlefield Trust, "The Capture and Burning of Washington, D.C.," www.battlefields.org.
101. Gleig, *Campaigns of the British Army*, 69. The siege and subsequent destruction of San Sebastian occurred while Gleig was serving in the British army in northern Spain. Like the public buildings in Washington, D.C., San Sebastian was burned almost entirely to the ground.

Chapter 22

102. Patterson, *Generals*, 181.
103. Patterson, *Generals*, 179–80.
104. Latour, *Historical Memoir*, 189. Letter from Jean Laffite to Mr. Blanque, September 4, 1814.

Chapter 23

105. Smith, "Preventing the 'Eggs of Insurrection,'" 87.
106. Smith, "Preventing the 'Eggs of Insurrection,'" 87.
107. Dale, *Staff Ride Handbook*, location 1,043.
108. Dale, *Staff Ride Handbook*, location 1,053.

Chapter 24

109. Gleig, *Campaigns of the British Army*, 89.
110. Gleig, *Campaigns of the British Army*, 90.
111. Gleig, *Campaigns of the British Army*, 93.
112. Gleig, *Campaigns of the British Army*, 81.

Chapter 25

113. American Battlefield Trust, "Battles of Fort Bowyer."
114. Owsley, *Struggle*, 110.
115. Owsley, *Struggle*, 110.
116. Owsley, *Struggle*, 110.

Chapter 26

117. Davis, *Pirates Laffite*, 186.
118. The only boats to survive the attack were small craft and pirogues. The ships that threatened the Gulf had been either burned or captured. Patterson's victory was complete.
119. The equivalent of $6.4 million in 2025.

Chapter 27

120. Chapman, *But for a Piece of Wood*, 28.
121. Cochrane's plan can be found in Owsley, *Struggle*, 134, 137.

Chapter 28

122. Owsley, *Struggle*, 40.
123. Owsley, *Struggle*, 81.
124. Owsley, *Struggle*, 100.
125. Owsley, *Struggle*, 118.

Chapter 29

126. Gleig, *Campaigns of the British Army*, 112.
127. Gleig, *Campaigns of the British Army*, 112.
128. Gleig, *Campaigns of the British Army*, 113.

129. Gleig, *Campaigns of the British Army*, 115–16.
130. Gleig, *Campaigns of the British Army*, 118.
131. Gleig, *Campaigns of the British Army*, 119.

Chapter 30

132. Davis, *Pirates Laffite*, 208–9.

Chapter 31

133. Bean, *Memoir*, 39.
134. Bean, *Memoir*, 48–52.

Chapter 32

135. Davis, *Greatest Fury*, 60.
136. Davis, *Greatest Fury*, 63–64.
137. Davis, *Greatest Fury*, 64.

Chapter 33

138. Davis, *Pirates Laffite*, 211.
139. Davis, *Pirates Laffite*, 213–14.
140. Davis, *Pirates Laffite*, 212.

Chapter 34

141. Two hundred of the 1st and 5th West Indian regiments died of cold on Pea Island and the boat trip (Pickles, *New Orleans 1815*, 48).
142. Patterson, *Generals*, 195.
143. Patterson, *Generals*, 197.
144. Davis, *Greatest Fury*, 83–84.
145. Davis, *Greatest Fury*, 89.
146. Patterson, *Generals*, 197–99.
147. Davis, *Greatest Fury*, 90.
148. Davis, *Greatest Fury*, 91.

Chapter 35

149. Davis, *Greatest Fury*, 91, 95.
150. Davis, *Greatest Fury*, 94.
151. Davis, *Greatest Fury*, 91.
152. Davis, *Greatest Fury*, 95.
153. Patterson, *Generals*, 203–4.
154. Davis, *Greatest Fury*, 97–99.
155. De Grummond, *Baratarians*, 88.
156. De Grummond, *Baratarians*, 90.
157. Patterson, *Generals*, 203–4.
158. Davis, *Greatest Fury*, 103.
159. Davis, *Greatest Fury*, 103–7.
160. Latour, *Historical Memoir*, 227.
161. Remini, *Battle of New Orleans*, 75.
162. Pickles, *New Orleans 1815*, 48.
163. Pickles, *New Orleans 1815*, 45.
164. De Grummond, *Baratarians*, 92.
165. Remini, *Battle of New Orleans*, 76.
166. Remini, *Battle of New Orleans*, 76–77.
167. De Grummond, *Baratarians*, 94.
168. Davis, *Greatest Fury*, 109.
169. Davis, *Greatest Fury*, 115–16.
170. Remini, *Battle of New Orleans*, 75–76.
171. Remini, *Battle of New Orleans*, 78–79.
172. De Grummond, *Baratarians*, 93.
173. De Grummond, *Baratarians*, 94–95.
174. Latour, *Historical Memoir*, 83.

Chapter 36

175. Remini, *Battle of New Orleans*, 89.
176. Pickles, *New Orleans 1815*, 51.
177. Patterson, *Generals*, 216.
178. De Grummond, *Baratarians*, 103.
179. Remini, *Battle of New Orleans*, 90–91.
180. Remini, *Battle of New Orleans*, 91.
181. Patterson, *Generals*, 217.
182. Patterson, *Generals*, 217; Davis, *Greatest Fury*, 139.

183. Remini, *Battle of New Orleans*, 91.
184. Remini, *Battle of New Orleans*, 89.
185. Remini, *Battle of New Orleans*, 93.
186. De Grummond, *Baratarians*, 101–2.
187. Garrigoux, *Visionary Adventurer*, 129.
188. Remini, *Battle of New Orleans*, 93–94.
189. Patterson, *Generals*, 218.
190. Remini, *Battle of New Orleans*, 94.
191. Owsley, *Struggle for the Gulf Borderlands*, 148.
192. Patterson, *Generals*, 218.
193. Pickles, *New Orleans 1815*, 53.
194. Remini, *Battle of New Orleans*, 95.
195. De Grummond, *Baratarians*, 107.
196. Latour, *Historical Memoir*, 89.
197. Remini, *Battle of New Orleans*, 95–96.
198. Latour, *Historical Memoir*, 88.
199. Davis, *Greatest Fury*, 151.
200. Patterson, *Generals*, 219–20.
201. Remini, *Battle of New Orleans*, 96.
202. De Grummond, *Baratarians*, 108.
203. Remini, *Battle of New Orleans*, 96–97.
204. Remini, *Battle of New Orleans*, 97.
205. Remini, *Battle of New Orleans*, 97.

Chapter 37

206. Pickles, *New Orleans 1815*, 58; Hickey, *Glorious Victory*, 105.
207. Pickles, *New Orleans 1815*, 150.
208. Pickles, *New Orleans 1815*, 58, 59.
209. Owsley, *Struggle*, 149.
210. Owsley, *Struggle*, 150.
211. Remini, *Battle of New Orleans*, 105.
212. Remini, *Battle of New Orleans*, 106–7.
213. Remini, *Battle of New Orleans*, 107.
214. Remini, *Battle of New Orleans*, 106.
215. Pickles, *New Orleans 1815*, 59; Remini, *Battle of New Orleans*, 108; Latour, *Historical Memoir*, 95.
216. Hickey, *Glorious Victory*, 134.
217. Davis, *Greatest Fury*, 187.

218. Remini, *Battle of New Orleans*, 109.
219. Davis, *Pirates Laffite*, 217.
220. Davis, *Greatest Fury*, 187.
221. Latour, *Historical Memoir*, 96.
222. Latour, *Historical Memoir*, 96.
223. Lieutenant Colonel Edward B. Cummings, "E Pluribus, Unum: The American Battle Line at New Orleans, 8 January 1815," The Army Historical Foundation, www.armyhistory.org.
224. BattleofNewOrleans.org, "The Battle of New Years Day, Jan. 1, 1815, The Artillery Duel," www.battleofneworleans.org.
225. Remini, *Battle of New Orleans*, 111; Fabric Link, "Burn Test."
226. Latour, *Historical Memoir*, 96.
227. Latour, *Historical Memoir*, 97.
228. Remini, *Battle of New Orleans*, 113.
229. Remini, *Battle of New Orleans*, 114.
230. Remini, *Battle of New Orleans*, 113.
231. Remini, *Battle of New Orleans*, 115.
232. Owsley, *Struggle*, 151.

Chapter 38

233. Hickey, *Glorious Victory*, 105; Remini, *Battle of New Orleans*, 130–31.
234. Pickles, *New Orleans 1815*, 61; Remini, *Battle of New Orleans*, 130–31.
235. Ironically, Pakenham's chief engineer at the Battle of New Orleans was Colonel John Fox Burgoyne, the illegitimate son of General John Burgoyne of Saratoga infamy.
236. Pickles, *New Orleans 1815*, 61.
237. Pickles, *New Orleans 1815*, 61; Remini, *Battle of New Orleans*, 83.
238. Remini, *Battle of New Orleans*, 123.
239. Davis, *Greatest Fury*, 218–19.
240. Davis, *Greatest Fury*, 219; Arsène Lacarrière-Latour, "War of 1812: 'To Describe Those Lines,'" American Battlefield Trust, www.battlefields.org.
241. Remini, *Battle of New Orleans*, 133.
242. Remini, *Battle of New Orleans*, 119–20.
243. Remini, *Battle of New Orleans*, 133.
244. Remini, *Battle of New Orleans*, 137.
245. Remini, *Battle of New Orleans*, 137.
246. Remini, *Battle of New Orleans*, 128.
247. Remini, *Battle of New Orleans*, 133–34.

248. Pickles, *New Orleans 1815*, 69.
249. Davis, *Greatest Fury*, 225–26.
250. Remini, *Battle of New Orleans*, 138.
251. Remini, *Battle of New Orleans*, 138.
252. Remini, *Battle of New Orleans*, 131.
253. Hickey, *Glorious Victory*, 3.
254. Remini, *Battle of New Orleans*, 138.
255. Remini, *Battle of New Orleans*, 141.
256. Remini, *Battle of New Orleans*, 140.
257. Pickles, *New Orleans 1815*, 70.
258. Pickles, *New Orleans 1815*, 70.
259. Pickles, *New Orleans 1815*, 71.
260. Davis, *Greatest Fury*, 244.
261. Pickles, *New Orleans 1815*, 73.
262. Pickles, *New Orleans 1815*, 73.
263. Pickles, *New Orleans 1815*, 74–75.
264. Remini, *Battle of New Orleans*, 159.
265. Davis, *Greatest Fury*, 268.
266. Pickles, *New Orleans 1815*, 76–80.
267. Davis, *Pirates Laffite*, 219.
268. Remini, *Battle of New Orleans*, 166.
269. Remini, *Battle of New Orleans*, 167–68.
270. Remini, *Battle of New Orleans*, 167.
271. Groom, *Patriotic Fire*, 212.
272. Groom, *Patriotic Fire*, 215.
273. Davis, *Greatest Fury*, 296.
274. Remini, *Battle of New Orleans*, 167.
275. Kilmeade and Yaeger, *Andrew Jackson*, 204.
276. Patterson, *Generals*, 251.

Chapter 39

277. Groom, *Patriotic Fire*, 216.
278. Groom, *Patriotic Fire*, 216.
279. Latour, *Historical Memoir*, 129–33, 250.
280. Remini, *Battle of New Orleans*, 178.
281. Remini, *Battle of New Orleans*, 179–80.

Chapter 40

282. The treaty had been signed—pending ultimate British ratification—and sent across the ocean on December 24, just as Jackson was concentrating and fortifying his troops along the Rodriguez Canal.

BIBLIOGRAPHY

Books

Aitchison, Robert. *A British Eyewitness at the Battle of New Orleans: The Memoir of Royal Navy Admiral Robert Aitchison, 1808–1827*. The Historic New Orleans Collection, 2004.

Allende, Isabel. *Island Beneath the Sea: A Novel*. HarperCollins, 2010.

Bean, Ellis P. *Memoir of Colonel Ellis P. Bean, Written by Himself, About the Year 1816*. Republished from Appendix II. In *History of Texas from Its First Settlement in 1685 to Its Annexation to the United States in 1846*. Vol. 1. Redfield, 1856.

Bunn, Mike. *Fourteenth Colony: The Forgotten Story of the Gulf South During America's Revolutionary Era*. NewSouth Books, 2020.

Chapman, Ron. *But for a Piece of Wood: The Battle of New Orleans*. Pelican Publishing, 2014.

Dale, Matthew B. *The Staff Ride Handbook for the Battles of New Orleans, 23 December 1814–8 January 1815*. Combat Studies Institute Press, U.S. Army Combined Arms Center, 2015.

Davis, William C. *The Greatest Fury: The Battle of New Orleans and the Rebirth of America*. Caliber, 2019.

———. *The Pirates Laffite: The Treacherous World of the Corsairs of the Gulf Coast*. Harcourt Books, 2005.

———. *The Rogue Republic: How Would-Be Patriots Waged the Shortest Revolution in American History*. Houghton Mifflin Harcourt, 2011.

De Grummond, Jane Lucas. *The Baratarians and the Battle of New Orleans*. Louisiana State University Press, 1961.

Foreman, Nicholas. "History of the United States' First Refugee Crises." *Smithsonian*, January 5, 2016.

Garrigoux, Jean. *A Visionary Adventurer: Arsène Lacarrière-Latour, 1778–1837, the Unusual Travels of a Frenchman in the Americas*. University of Louisiana at Lafayette Press, 2017.

Gleig, George Robert. *The Campaigns of the British Army at Washington and New Orleans*. Good Press, 2022.

Grocott, Terence. *Shipwrecks of the Revolutionary & Napoleonic Eras*. Chatham, 1997.

Groom, Winston. *Patriotic Fire: Andrew Jackson and Jean Laffite at the Battle Of New Orleans*. Vintage Books, 2007.

Heaney, Sister Jane Frances, O.S.U. *A Century of Pioneering: A History of the Ursuline Nuns in New Orleans 1727–1827*. Ursuline Sisters of New Orleans, 1993.

Hickey, Donald R. *Glorious Victory: Andrew Jackson and the Battle of New Orleans*. John Hopkins University Press, 2015.

Kilmeade, Brian, and Don Yaeger. *Andrew Jackson and the Miracle of New Orleans*. Sentinel, 2017.

———. *Thomas Jefferson and the Tripoli Pirates: The Forgotten War That Changed American History*. Sentinel, 2015.

Latour, Arsène Lacarrière. *Historical Memoir of the War in West Florida and Louisiana in 1814–1815, with an Atlas*. The University Press of Florida, 1999.

Owsley, Frank Lawrence. *Struggle for the Gulf Borderlands: The Creek War and the Battle of New Orleans, 1812–1815*. University of Alabama Press, 2000.

Patterson, Benton Rain. *The Generals: Andrew Jackson, Sir Edward Pakenham, and the Road to the Battle of New Orleans*. New York University Press, 2005.

Pickles, Tim. *New Orleans 1815: Andrew Jackson Crushes the British*. Osprey Publishing, 1993.

Remini, Robert V. *The Battle of New Orleans: Andrew Jackson and America's First Military Victory*. Viking Group, 1999.

Saxon, Lyle. *Fabulous New Orleans*. Pelican Publishing Company, 1988.

Turnbow, Tony. *Hardened to Hickory: The Missing Chapter in Andrew Jackson's Life*. Tony L. Turnbow, 2018.

Online Sources

American Battlefield Trust. www.battlefields.org.

American Heritage. www.americanheritage.com.

The Army Historical Foundation. www.armyhistory.org.

BattleofNewOrleans.org. www.battleofneworleans.org.

Fabric Link. "Burn Test." www.fabriclink.com.

"Gen. Sir Edward Nicolls, K.C.B." *The Gentleman's Magazine and Historical Review* 218 (January–June 1865): 644–46. www.babel.hathitrust.org.

Naval History and Heritage Command. "Daniel Todd Patterson, 6 March 1786–25 August 1839." www.history.navy.mil.

New Orleans. www.myneworleans.com.

Owlcation. www.owlcation.com.

Shannon Selin. www.shannonselin.com.

Smith, Gene Allan. "Preventing the 'Eggs of Insurrection' from Hatching: The U.S. Navy and Control of the Mississippi River, 1806–1815." Canadian Nautical Research Society. www.cnrs-scrn.org.

Three Decks. www.threedecks.org.

U.S. Customs and Border Protection. www.cbp.gov.

U.S. Environmental Protection Agency. www.epa.gov.

Vallar, Cindy. "Scottish Pirates." *Pirates and Privateers: A History of Maritime Piracy.* www.cindyvallar.com.

Newspapers

Alexandria Gazette

Daily Universal Register

Statesman and Gazette (Natchez)

ABOUT THE AUTHOR

Ryan Starrett was born and raised in Jackson, Mississippi. He has written and coauthored, along with his friend Josh Foreman, a dozen other books dealing with the history of Mississippi and the Deep South. Their work can be perused at foremanstarrett.com.